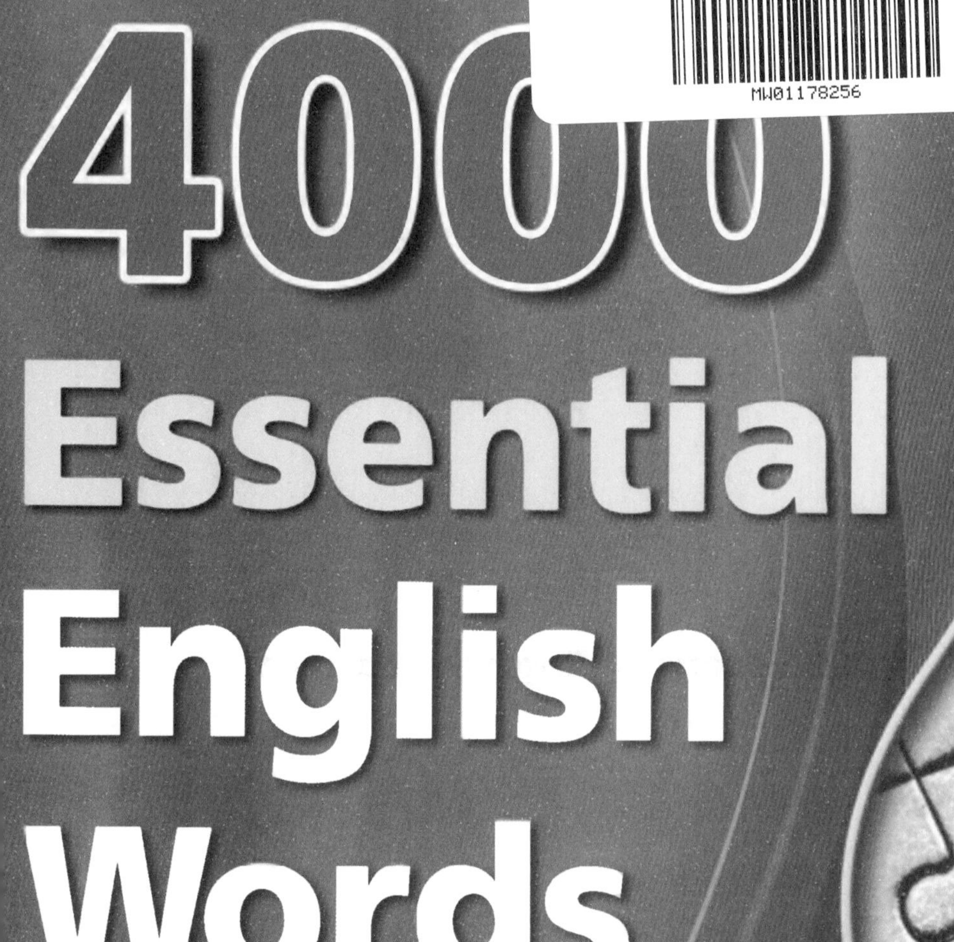

4000 Essential English Words

5

Paul Nation

4000 Essential English Words 5

4000 Essential English Words 5

Paul Nation

Acquisitions Editor: Fidel Cruz
Project Coordinator: Annie Cho
Design: Design Plus

email: info@compasspub.com
http://www.compasspub.com

ISBN: 978-1-59966-406-4

10 9 8 7 6 5 4
12 11

Photo Credits

All images © Shutterstock, Inc.

Table of Contents

Introduction

About the Vocabulary

The 600 words in each book of this series along with the additional target words presented in the appendices included in the first three books of the series are the most useful words in English. They were found by analysis of a collection of English course books from various levels in the primary, secondary and tertiary school systems. The words included in this series were chosen because they occurred many times in different levels of these materials. Because of the way
that they were chosen, these words have the following characteristics:

1 They are useful in both spoken and written English. No matter what English course you are studying, the words in these books will be of value to you.

2 Each word in these books is a high-frequency word. This means that the effort in learning the words is well repaid by the number of times learners have a chance to encounter or use them.

3 These books as a whole cover a large proportion of the words in any spoken or written text. They cover at least 80% of the words in newspapers and academic texts, and at least 90% of the words in novels. They also cover at least 90% of the words in conversation.

About the Books

The activities in these books are specially designed to make use of important learning conditions. Firstly, the words are introduced using sentence definitions and an example sentence. The activities that follow in the units encourage learners to recall the meanings and forms of the words. Some activities also make the learners think about the meaning of the words in the context of a sentence—a sentence different from the sentences that occurred in the introduction of the words. Moreover, each unit ends with a story containing the target words. While reading the story, the learners have to recall the meanings of the words and suit them to the context of the story. Such activities help learners develop a better understanding of a common meaning for a given word which fits the different uses.

Illustrations for each target word are provided to help learners visualize the word as it is being used in the example sentence. These word/image associations aim to help students grasp the meaning of the word as well as recall the word later.

It should be noted that words have more than one grammatical category. However, this series focuses on the word's most common form. This is mentioned to remind learners that just because a word is labeled and utilized as a noun in this series does not mean that it can never be used in another form such as an adjective. This series has simply focused on the word in the form that it is most likely to be expressed.

Supporting Learning with Outside Activities

A well-balanced language course provides four major opportunities for learning: learning through input, learning through output, deliberate learning, and fluency development. The highly structured activities in these books support all four types of learning opportunities. In addition, learning can further be supported through the following activities:

1 Have students create vocabulary cards with one word from the unit on one side of the card and the translation of the word in the student's first language on the other side. Students should use the cards for study in free moments during the day. Over several weeks, students will find that quick repeated studying for brief periods of time is more effective than studying for hours at one sitting.

2 Assign graded readers at students' appropriate levels. Reading such books provides both enjoyment as well as meaning-focused input which will help the words stick in students' memory.

3 Practice reading fluency to promote faster recall of word meaning for both sight recognition and usage. Compass Publishing's *Reading for Speed and Fluency* is a good resource for reading fluency material.

4 Include listening, speaking, and writing activities in classes. Reinforcement of the high-frequency vocabulary presented in this series is important across all the four language skills.

Author **Paul Nation**

Paul Nation is professor of Applied Linguistics in the School of Linguistics and Applied Language Studies at Victoria University of Wellington, New Zealand. He has taught in Indonesia, Thailand, the United States, Finland, and Japan. His specialist interests are language teaching methodology and vocabulary learning.

UNIT 1

Word List

allot [əlάt] *v.*

To **allot** something means to give it to someone.

→ *The coach **allotted** each team five minutes to prepare a strategy.*

appall [əpɔ́:l] *v.*

To **appall** means to horrify, shock, or disgust someone.

→ *The boy was **appalled** when he saw the accident.*

cache [kæʃ] *n.*

A **cache** is a hiding place for valuable things.

→ *The pirates kept their jewelry in a **cache** hidden in a cave.*

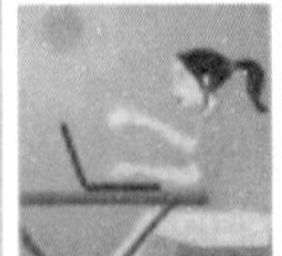

convenience [kənví:njəns] *n.*

Convenience is a state of being able to do something with little effort.

→ *The Internet allows consumers to shop at their own **convenience**.*

dearth [də:rθ] *n.*

A **dearth** is an amount or supply which is not large enough.

→ *There is a **dearth** of money in my bank account. I can't afford a new car.*

deliberate [dilíbərit] *adj.*

If a thing you do is **deliberate**, you intend to do it.

→ *She made a **deliberate** effort to save money each month.*

dire [daiər] *adj.*

When something is **dire**, it is terrible and very serious.

→ *The tornado created a **dire** situation for the small town.*

elapse [ilǽps] *v.*

To **elapse** means to pass, as in seconds, minutes, or hours.

→ *A few seconds must **elapse** before you can take another picture.*

empathy [émpəθi] *n.*

Empathy is sharing or understanding another person's feelings.

→ *The caring nurse had **empathy** for her patients.*

fanciful [fǽnsifəl] *adj.*

When something is **fanciful**, it is unusual or unrealistic.

→ *The girl had **fanciful** ideas about doing well in school without studying.*

gripe [graip] *v.*

To **gripe** means to complain constantly.

→ *Lawrence always **gripes** when he has to do chores.*

grueling [grú:əliŋ] *adj.*

When something is **grueling**, it is very hard to do.

→ *The climber faced the **grueling** task of reaching the top of the steep mountain.*

mundane [mʌ́ndein] *adj.*

When something is **mundane**, it is boring, common, or ordinary.

→ *The man had the **mundane** chore of raking thousands of leaves into piles.*

opt [ɑpt] *v.*

To **opt** is to make a choice, especially when deciding in favor of something.

→ *My brother likes chocolate ice cream, but I always **opt** for vanilla.*

outrage [autrèidʒ] *n.*

Outrage is a very strong emotion of anger or shock.

→ *Tommy was feeling **outrage** when his parents said he couldn't go to the dance.*

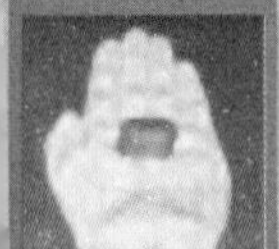

paltry [pɔ́:ltri] *adj.*

When an amount of something is **paltry**, it is very small.

→ *The poor man had a **paltry** sum of money.*

rectify [réktəfài] *v.*

To **rectify** something means to correct it.

→ *I quickly **rectified** the spelling mistakes that I had on my essay.*

resourceful [ri:sɔ́:rsfəl] *adj.*

When someone is **resourceful**, they are good at dealing with hard situations.

→ *After his boat sunk, Matt was **resourceful** enough to build a raft.*

sustenance [sʌ́stənəns] *n.*

Sustenance is food and water needed to keep a person, animal, or plant alive.

→ *Without the proper **sustenance**, the man will starve.*

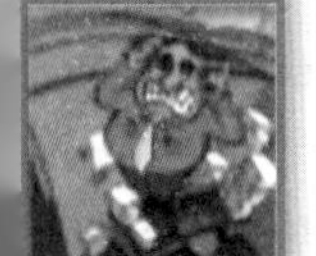

tedious [tí:diəs] *adj.*

When something is **tedious**, it is long, frustrating, and boring.

→ *His job involved a lot of **tedious** typing, filing, and organizing.*

Exercise 1

Choose the answer that best fits the question.

1. You would have empathy if you _______.
   a. shared sad feelings b. lost in a game c. hurt your arm d. ate a large meal
2. How would you feel if there was a dearth of food?
   a. Happy b. Hungry c. Full d. Sleepy
3. If something is a convenience, then it makes _______.
   a. you very angry b. you feel sick c. a lot of money d. a task easier
4. How would a resourceful person deal with a problem?
   a. Ignore it b. Give up c. Cry and ask for help d. Find a solution
5. If something was deliberate, then it was _______.
   a. done with pride b. done easily c. done on purpose d. not done at all
6. How would you describe someone feeling a sense of outrage?
   a. Peaceful b. Upset c. Tired d. Arrogant
7. What fanciful idea might a doctor have?
   a. Give a patient medicine b. Be kind to them
   c. Tell them to rest d. Ask a fairy for advice
8. What would a tired person likely opt to do?
   a. Watch a movie b. Exercise c. Finish a book d. Go to bed
9. To rectify hurting your friend, you would _______.
   a. say sorry b. laugh at him c. hit him d. ignore him
10. What might appall a teacher?
    a. Smart students b. A happy student c. A mean attitude d. A long test

Exercise 2

Choose the one that is similar in meaning to the given word.

1. outrage
   a. idea b. anger c. beauty d. personality
2. rectify
   a. to correct b. to sadden c. to bore d. to be hard
3. sustenance
   a. belief b. flowing c. food and drink d. torn
4. dire
   a. terrible b. likely c. large d. small
5. opt
   a. to remove b. to yell c. to shout d. to choose

Exercise 3

Choose the one that is opposite in meaning to the given word.

1. tedious
   a. fun b. to read c. to shrink d. to love

2. appall
   a. to greet b. to lower c. to please d. to create

3. paltry
   a. worthless b. large c. ugly d. absent

4. grueling
   a. rough b. exact c. easy d. necessary

5. resourceful
   a. foolish b. realistic c. impressive d. surprising

Exercise 4

Write C if the italicized word is used correctly. Write I if the word is used incorrectly.

1. ____ I had a big breakfast. Many hours will *elapse* before I feel hungry again.

2. ____ Dan was a nice man, but no one would work for him because of his *fanciful* ideas.

3. ____ I was very grateful for my birthday gifts. I *griped* about them to all of my friends.

4. ____ Because there was a *dearth* of food at home, the family went out to eat.

5. ____ The puppy was happy to learn new tricks. Each one was very *mundane* for him.

6. ____ Mother *allotted* me and my brother the money. Now she had all the money.

7. ____ The boy was proud of his trophies. He displayed them in a *cache* for everyone to see.

8. ____ Because he had planned for the trap to capture his victim, he was very *deliberate*.

9. ____ The violent criminal was on the news this evening. His actions *appalled* most people.

10. ____ That man is very selfish. He has *empathy* for every person he meets.

The Little Mice

Beth was a very **resourceful** and conservative mouse. She knew that winter was coming and that there would soon be a **dearth** of food. So she decided to make gathering food for winter her primary job. Gathering food was a **grueling** and **mundane** activity, but Beth made a **deliberate** effort because she knew that it was important. She **allotted** herself a few hours every day to collect beans. By winter, she had collected a massive pile and hid them in a **cache**.

Beth had a sister named Mary. Mary lacked ambition. She had **fanciful** ideas about how she would survive winter. She thought that food would just come to her and that she could work at her own **convenience**. She **opted** to spend the days playing and dancing, instead of gathering beans. When the final hours of autumn **elapsed**, Mary had only a **paltry** amount of food stored away.

Mary realized that her food supply was too small to last through winter. She visited her sister. Mary said, "Beth, I am in a **dire** situation. I didn't gather enough food for winter. Will you let me share your beans? Please have some **empathy** for your sister!"

Beth thought for a moment. Then she replied, "Mary, I am truly sorry for you. But I will not give you any of my beans. Instead, I will let you have my empty bag. You can still work hard and gather enough food for the winter. It will be **tedious**, but you will learn the value of hard work."

Beth's words **appalled** Mary. Mary cried with **outrage**, "There is too much work! I won't have any time to dance or play!"

Beth said, "It is crucial that you gather enough food. You must have **sustenance** before you have fun. Go now, and **rectify** your situation."

Mary **griped** some more, but she knew that her sister was right. She took the bag and went to work gathering her own beans for the winter.

Reading Comprehension

PART A Mark each statement T for true or F for false. Rewrite the false statements to make them true.

1. ____ Beth was resourceful and conservative, so she gathered a paltry pile of beans for her cache.

____

2. ____ Because gathering food was tedious, Beth allotted a few hours of every day to do it.

____

3. ____ Beth did grueling and mundane work to overcome the dearth of food in the winter.

____

4. ____ Beth's reply appalled Mary and made her reply in outrage.

____

5. ____ When the hours of autumn elapsed, Mary had a massive amount of food.

____

PART B Answer the questions.

1. What was Beth's primary job?

____

____

2. What fanciful idea did Mary opt to try?

____

____

3. What did Mary want her sister to have empathy about?

____

____

4. How did Mary rectify her dire situation and get sustenance?

____

____

5. Even though she griped, what did Mary know at the end of the story?

____

____

UNIT 2

Word List

abbey [æbi] *n.*

An **abbey** is a house or group of houses where monks or nuns live.

→ *When the monk returned to the **abbey**, he went immediately to his bedroom.*

abundant [əbʌ́ndənt] *adj.*

If something is **abundant**, then it is available in large quantities.

→ *Cakes, cookies, and candy were so **abundant** that the child was very happy.*

adjoin [ədʒɔ́in] *v.*

To **adjoin** something means to be next to or attached to something else.

→ *She can listen to her brother's conversations because her room **adjoins** his.*

ample [ǽmpl] *adj.*

If something is **ample**, then it is enough or more than enough.

→ *There was an **ample** supply of oats to feed the horses.*

arid [ǽrid] *adj.*

If a place is **arid**, then it is hot and dry and gets very little or no rain.

→ *Not many plants grow in the **arid** desert.*

cathedral [kəəí:drəl] *n.*

A **cathedral** is an important and often large and beautifully built church.

→ *The large **cathedral** is full of people on Sunday mornings.*

deprive [dipráiv] *v.*

To **deprive** someone of something means to not let them have it.

→ *Because the child was bad, she was **deprived** of her dessert after dinner.*

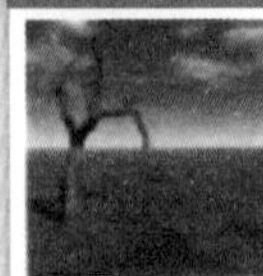

drought [draut] *n.*

A **drought** is a long period of time in which little or no rain falls.

→ *After three months of **drought**, the vegetation and trees started dying.*

eligible [élidʒəbəl] *adj.*

If someone is **eligible**, then they are permitted to do or have something.

→ *Only people who bought tickets were **eligible** to win a prize.*

fast [fæst] *v.*

To **fast** means to go without food or drink for a period of time.

→ *In her religion, they **fast** for five days and then have a big feast.*

grumble [grʌ́mbəl] *v.*

To **grumble** means to complain.

→ *He **grumbled** about having to work late on Friday.*

inland [ínlənd] *adv.*

If someone goes **inland,** they travel into the center of a country or land.

→ *The river curved **inland** near the campground.*

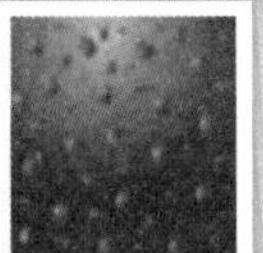

moisture [mɔ́istʃər] *n.*

Moisture is small drops of water in the air or on a surface.

→ *If you breathe on a window, **moisture** from your breath collects on the glass.*

nonetheless [nʌ̀nðəlés] *adv.*

If something happens **nonetheless,** then it occurs despite some other thing.

→ *She tried to keep the dog out of the mud, but it got dirty **nonetheless**.*

oath [ouθ] *n.*

An **oath** is a formal, often public, promise.

→ *Judges must take an **oath** to be fair to everyone in court.*

prairie [prɛ́əri] *n.*

A **prairie** is a large flat area of grassland.

→ *The **prairie** was perfect for a farm because there were hills and trees.*

ragged [rǽgid] *adj.*

If something is **ragged,** then it is old, torn, and falling apart.

→ *They could see his toes through the holes in his **ragged** shoes.*

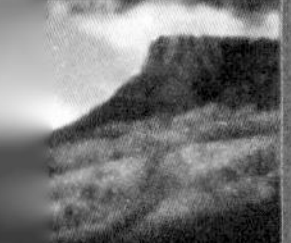

rugged [rʌ́gid] *adj.*

If an area of land is **rugged,** then it is rocky and difficult to travel through.

→ *Their car couldn't make it far along the **rugged** roads.*

scarce [skɛəːrs] *adj.*

If something is **scarce,** then it is in a very small amount.

→ *When gasoline was **scarce,** we rode our bikes, instead of driving, to school.*

speculate [spékjəlèit] *v.*

To **speculate** means to guess about something.

→ *My sister looked at the sky and **speculated** that it would rain tomorrow.*

Exercise 1

Choose the answer that best fits the question.

1. What would probably happen if you deprived someone of food?
   a. They could die.
   b. They could feel relieved.
   c. They could feel happy.
   d. They could feel peace.

2. A rugged surface would feel _______.
   a. very rough
   b. smooth
   c. cool and slippery
   d. warm and hard

3. If you were speculating about something, you would be doing what?
   a. Stating a fact
   b. Looking for truth
   c. Making a speech
   d. Making a guess

4. Where would someone take an oath?
   a. At the subway
   b. In court
   c. On vacation
   d. In their sleep

5. If something were covered with moisture, then it would feel _______.
   a. hard
   b. rough
   c. soft
   d. wet

Exercise 2

Fill in the blanks with the correct words from the word bank.

Word Bank

abundant	moisture	cathedral	scarce	fast
arid	eligible	oath	rugged	prairie

Traveling across the 1_____________ was more difficult than it seemed.
The ground was very 2_____________, and the grass was high.

John had been in a place with a(n) 3_____________ climate for a long time.
He forgot that in a humid place everything was covered with 4_____________.

The people who attend that church 5_____________ for two weeks in March.
Then they go to the 6_____________ where they pray and eat a small meal of soup.

We didn't know what to do with such a(n) 7_____________ supply of wood.
We had gotten used to making small fires when it was so 8_____________.

In order for the students to attend the dance, they had to take a(n) 9_____________.
Those that didn't promise to be on their best behavior were not 10_____________.

Exercise 3

Write C if the italicized word is used correctly. Write I if the word is used incorrectly.

1. ____ Climbing up the *prairie* was more difficult without the help of ropes.
2. ____ There was no way he could mend the holes in his shirt. It was too *rugged* to wear.
3. ____ In some countries, only people who owned land were *eligible* to vote.
4. ____ The capital was in the middle of the country. They had to travel *inland* to get there.
5. ____ He knew she didn't like him, but he helped her *nonetheless*.

Exercise 4

Write a word that is similar in meaning to the underlined part.

1. That part of the country is so <u>hot and dry</u> that no one lives there.

   ____

2. After getting off the boat, they took a train <u>toward the center of the country</u>.

   ____

3. They survived through the <u>time in which no rain fell</u> by carrying water down from the hills.

   ____

4. This <u>house for the monks</u> was built well over 200 years ago.

   ____

5. He knew he'd get in trouble, but he stole the money <u>despite the punishment</u>.

   ____

6. He <u>guessed</u> that the visitor's team would win the game.

   ____

7. The number of people helping to clean the trash near the river was <u>more than enough</u>.

   ____

8. There was a small park that <u>was next to</u> the yard surrounding the church.

   ____

9. Because his pants were <u>old and torn</u>, Dad bought him a new pair.

   ____

10. The long lines <u>did not allow</u> her of a chance to buy a ticket for the concert.

   ____

The Helpful Abbey

It had not rained on the **prairie** for several months. Because of the **drought**, the climate had become very **arid**. There was no **moisture** left in the soil. No crops could grow in the dry ground. By wintertime, the people had nothing to eat.

The hungry families heard about an **abbey** near the mountains where food and water was still **abundant**. So they traveled **inland**, across the prairie, to the abbey.

At first only a few families arrived, seeking food and shelter. Then there was **ample** food. The monks fed them and let them sleep in the small **cathedral**.

Soon, however, more families were arriving every day. These people had to travel farther, so they were in worse condition. The **rugged** journey had made their clothes **ragged**. They were cold and tired. The tiny cathedral was soon full.

Food became **scarce**. The monks began to **grumble**. They began to **speculate** that there would be no food. "If more families come, we won't make it through the winter," said a young monk. "We must ask some of them to leave."

The abbot heard this. "We cannot do that," he said. "It would be wrong to **deprive** them of food and shelter. We took an **oath** to help those that need help. All here are in need, so all are **eligible** to receive our food and shelter."

"But we won't have enough," the monk said.

"That might be true, but we must help them **nonetheless**. We will **fast**," the abbot replied. "Also, we will give our rooms in the abbey to those sleeping outside, and we will sleep in the churchyard that **adjoins** the cathedral."

The monks were reluctant at first, but they did what the oldest monk said. By the end of winter, there was still enough food and shelter for everyone. They learned that sometimes helping others means you must give more help than you first expected.

Reading Comprehension

PART A Mark each statement T for true or F for false. Rewrite the false statements to make them true.

1. ____ The moisture in the soil was gone because a drought made the prairie become arid.

2. ____ The hungry families traveled inland to an abbey that still had abundant food.

3. ____ Food was scarce, but the monks had to deprive the families nonetheless.

4. ____ At first there was ample food and enough room in the cathedral for everyone.

5. ____ The rugged journey to the abbey had left many people's clothing looking ragged.

PART B Answer the questions.

1. According to the abbot, who was eligible to receive the monks' help?

2. When the monks grumbled, what did the young monk speculate would happen if more families arrived?

3. Why did the monks fast and sleep in the churchyard that adjoined the cathedral?

4. What was the oath that the monks had taken?

5. What did the monks learn about helping others?

UNIT 3

Word List

analytic [ǽnəlítik] *adj.*

If something is **analytic**, it is related to logic and reasoning.

→ *The **analytic** article criticized the new plan and presented one of its own.*

assert [əsə́:rt] *v.*

To **assert** a fact or belief means to state it with confidence.

→ *He **asserted** that his mother's cooking was better than his best friend's.*

bachelor [bǽtʃələr] *n.*

A **bachelor** is an unmarried man.

→ *Since he was a **bachelor**, Jason did his shopping by himself.*

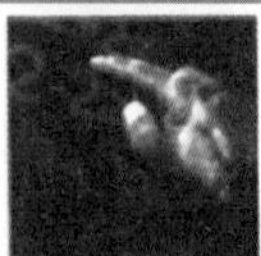

calculus [kǽlkjələs] *n.*

Calculus is an advanced type of mathematics.

→ *By using **calculus**, scientists determined small changes in the stars' brightness*

celestial [səléstʃəl] *adj.*

If something is **celestial**, it is related to the sky or to outer space.

→ *Comets are **celestial** objects that are rarely seen.*

cognitive [kɑ́gnətiv] *adj.*

If something is **cognitive**, it is related to learning and knowing things.

→ *After her physical examination, her **cognitive** strengths were tested.*

collision [kəlíʒən] *n.*

A **collision** is the act of two things hitting into each another.

→ *The **collision** between the two cars created a loud noise.*

competent [kámpətənt] *adj.*

If someone is **competent**, they are able to think or act successfully.

→ ***Competent** employees are much better than unknowledgeable ones.*

diploma [diplóumə] *n.*

A **diploma** is a certificate proving that someone has completed their studies.

→ *After four years of college, Mary finally had a **diploma**.*

excel [iksél] *v.*

To **excel** at a subject or activity means to be very good at it.

→ *Jenny **excels** at playing the piano.*

geology [dʒiːɑ́lədʒi] *n.*

Geology is the study of the Earth's natural structures and how they change.

→ *Because he studied **geology,** he knew how the mountains were formed.*

harness [hɑ́ːrnis] *v.*

To **harness** something means to control and use it, usually to make energy.

→ *The sails **harness** the wind in order to move.*

intellect [íntəlèkt] *n.*

An **intellect** is a person's ability to understand things easily.

→ *She was known for her quick and strong **intellect** as well as her beauty.*

keen [kiːn] *adj.*

If someone is **keen**, they are intelligent.

→ *Only the **keenest** of students could have solved that math problem.*

mythology [miθɑ́lədʒi] *n.*

Mythology is a group of stories from a particular country or region.

→ *Egyptian **mythology** was the basis for a religion.*

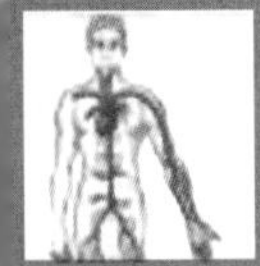

physiology [fiziɑ́lədʒi] *n.*

Physiology is the study of the various parts of living things.

→ *His work in **physiology** helped him understand how the human body works.*

radioactive [rèidiouǽktiv] *adj.*

If something is **radioactive,** then it lets out, or is related to, radiation.

→ ***Radioactive** materials can be very bad for anyone's health.*

relativity [rèlətívəti] *n.*

Relativity is a set of ideas about time and space developed by Albert Einstein.

→ ***Relativity** teaches that light travels at the same speed in the universe.*

sociology [sòusiɑ́lədʒi] *n.*

Sociology is the study of human society, its organizations, and problems.

→ ***Sociology** teaches that people's problems are a result of their society.*

theoretical [θìːərétikəl] *adj.*

If something is **theoretical,** it is based on theory rather than experience.

→ *His conclusion was only **theoretical** and not meant to be publicized.*

Exercise 1

Choose the answer that best fits the question.

1. What is geology the study of?
a. Earth's life forms
b. Earth's structures
c. Earth's orbit
d. Earth's atmosphere

2. In physiology, you would probably study something like ________.
a. the ocean's waves
b. the soil
c. time and space
d. parts of living things

3. Which of the following would NOT be considered celestial?
a. Stars
b. Comets
c. Navigation
d. Meteors

4. What else does sociology deal with besides people and their culture?
a. People's problems
b. Plant reproduction
c. Alien life forms
d. Ocean currents

5. If you excel at something, then that means you are ________.
a. incompetent
b. brave
c. literate
d. good at something

Exercise 2

Choose the one that is similar in meaning to the given word.

1. intellect
a. name
b. ability
c. speed
d. growth

2. calculus
a. content
b. religion
c. design
d. math

3. assert
a. state
b. explode
c. purchase
d. permit

4. cognitive
a. friendly
b. expensive
c. colorful
d. learning

5. diploma
a. money
b. mammal
c. license
d. tower

6. mythology
a. folklore
b. business
c. freedom
d. beauty

7. analytic
a. official
b. ancient
c. logical
d. patient

8. harness
a. use
b. expand
c. discover
d. insist

9. competent
a. brave
b. capable
c. handsome
d. broken

10. collision
a. hammer
b. scar
c. school
d. crash

Exercise 3

Write C if the italicized word is used correctly. Write I if the word is used incorrectly.

1. ____ In *physiology*, we studied various types of rock and the process that made them.
2. ____ She feared that if no one married her, she'd be a *bachelor* her entire life.
3. ____ Many old factories *harnessed* rivers and streams to power their equipment.
4. ____ Her knowledge of different societies came from her work in *sociology*.
5. ____ If the two bikes hadn't turned at the last moment, there would have been a *collision*.
6. ____ In *geology*, we learned about the importance of our bones.
7. ____ The only proof that the new rocket would work was *theoretical*.
8. ____ The car *excelled* every time he stepped on the gas pedal.
9. ____ Learning about *calculus* in my literature class was a really enjoyable time.
10. ____ The test proved that Mark was *keener* than his older brother Dave.

Exercise 4

Write a word that is similar in meaning to the underlined part.

1. She really learned a lot from just one class of the beliefs and stories of different cultures.

   ____

2. When he states the fact with confidence that flowers can grow here, you believe him.

   ____

3. The tests will prove whether or not his discovery is real and not just based on theory.

   ____

4. The dangerous thing about nuclear power is the radiation waste it produces.

   ____

5. John has good learning skills that have helped him in his studies.

   ____

6. The stars and moon in outer space objects lit the path so I could see where I was walking.

   ____

7. Having a certificate of completed studies will give him more options for the future.

   ____

8. Albert Einstein's ideas about time and space changed both science and the world.

   ____

9. You have to be very intelligent in order to solve this puzzle in a short amount of time.

   ____

0. Every day the unmarried men came to her home to see which of them she might choose.

   ____

The Bachelor's Lesson

A **keen** young **bachelor** had finished his studies at the university. As soon as he had received his **diploma**, he **asserted** to everyone he met that he was the smartest person in town.

"I **excel** at everything I study," he said, bragging about his knowledge. "I've mastered **calculus** and **physiology**. I even understand the great **theoretical** teachings of science, such as **relativity**. There is nothing that I don't know. Whether it's the movements of **celestial** objects, like planets and stars, or how to **harness** the power of **radioactive** substances, I know everything."

But actually, there was something the bachelor did not know. Though his **analytic** abilities were great, he failed to notice he was missing something very important in his life.

One day while walking through town, the bachelor witnessed a **collision** between two cars. Both drivers appeared to be injured, but the scholar only stood and watched.

He thought to himself, "Those idiots should have been more alert. They really must not be very **competent**." He never thought the drivers needed help.

"Please help me," said the female driver in a weak voice. "Help me, too," said the male driver. "I'm hurt and can't move."

Suddenly the bachelor realized he was the only person near the accident. He quit thinking and ran to help the drivers. He carefully helped them out of their vehicles and then called an ambulance.

The drivers were saved, and the bachelor felt the best he had in his entire life. Studying **mythology**, **sociology**, and **geology** didn't give him this wonderful feeling. It was the act of helping others, not his **cognitive** skills, that gave him this great feeling.

He had learned an important lesson. He learned that **intellect** isn't everything; being helpful is just as important. "Having only a brain is not enough," he thought. "You must also have a heart."

Reading Comprehension

PART A Mark each statement T for true or F for false. Rewrite the false statements to make them true.

1. ____ The bachelor excelled at calculus, physiology, and theoretical science, such as relativity.

   ____

2. ____ He knew the movements of radioactive materials and how to harness the power of celestial objects.

   ____

3. ____ The bachelor thought the drivers in the collision were not competent.

   ____

4. ____ Studying mythology, sociology, and geology gave the bachelor a wonderful feeling.

   ____

5. ____ The bachelor's intellect and not his cognitive talents had made him feel this great.

   ____

PART B Answer the questions.

1. What did the keen bachelor assert after receiving his diploma?

   ____

   ____

2. What happened while the bachelor was strolling through town?

   ____

   ____

3. How did the bachelor feel after saving the drivers?

   ____

   ____

4. Despite his analytic abilities, what did the bachelor fail to notice about his life?

   ____

   ____

5. Besides a brain, what did the bachelor realize was important to have in life?

   ____

   ____

UNIT 4

Word List

administrator [ædmínəstrèitər] *n.*

An **administrator** is a person who controls a business, company, or organization.
→ *Everyone in the store did whatever the **administrator** asked them to do.*

affluent [ǽflu(:)ənt] *adj.*

If someone is **affluent**, they are wealthy.
→ *People in the city are usually more **affluent** than people in the country.*

audit [ɔ́:dit] *v.*

To **audit** means to inspect financial records from a person or business.
→ *The government usually **audits** companies that report lower than usual incomes.*

automate [ɔ́:təmèit] *v.*

To **automate** a company means to install machines or computers to do the work.
→ *When the bank **automated**, it started installing ATM machines.*

bribe [braib] *v.*

To **bribe** someone means to illegally persuade them for a favor with money.
→ *The judge was **bribed** so that she would set the suspect free.*

corrupt [kərʌ́pt] *adj.*

If someone is **corrupt**, they break the law for money or fame.
→ *The **corrupt** policemen didn't arrest the man because he gave them money.*

dispose [dispóuz] *v.*

To **dispose** of something means to get rid of it.
→ *He **disposed** of the can by throwing it into the recycle bin.*

headquarters [hédkwɔ̀:rtərz] *n.*

A **headquarters** is a building where the bosses of a company work.
→ *He drove the long route to **headquarters** because it was a nice day.*

incentive [inséntiv] *n.*

An **incentive** is what makes a person want to do something.
→ *The chance of winning a prize was **incentive** to get people to play the game.*

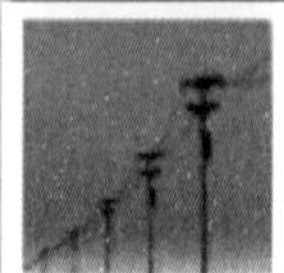

infrastructure [ínfrəstrʌ̀ktʃər] *n.*

An **infrastructure** is a collection of services needed to run a society or business.
→ *Power lines are important parts of a city's **infrastructure**.*

legislate [lédʒislèit] *v.*

To **legislate** means to make laws.

→ *Senators have to* ***legislate*** *fairly, so most people will enjoy the benefits.*

legitimate [lidʒitəmit] *adj.*

If something is **legitimate,** then it is acceptable according to the law.

→ *She found a* ***legitimate*** *plan to raise extra funds for her vacation.*

manipulate [mənipjəlèit] *v.*

To **manipulate** something means to skillfully or unfairly control or affect it.

→ *The Dr.* ***manipulated*** *the data to make it look like the cure was working.*

merchandise [mə́:rtʃəndàiz] *n.*

Merchandise is goods ready to be purchased or sold.

→ *The store added more* ***merchandise*** *because there were more shoppers.*

retail [rí:teil] *n.*

Retail is the activity of selling goods to the public, often for personal use.

→ *Though cheap to make, once a t-shirt reaches* ***retail,*** *it costs ten times as much.*

revenue [rèvənjù:] *n.*

Revenue is the income made by a company.

→ *The new products really increased the business's monthly* ***revenue.***

rubbish [rʌ́biʃ] *n.*

Rubbish is trash or waste.

→ *The floor around the garbage can was covered with all kinds of* ***rubbish.***

subsidy [sʌ́bsidi] *n.*

A **subsidy** is money given by the government to companies to assist them.

→ *The official gave the company a* ***subsidy,*** *so it could open two new factories.*

transaction [trænsǽkʃən] *n.*

A **transaction** is an act of buying or selling something.

→ *Because the clerk was new at the job, the simple* ***transaction*** *took a long time.*

violate [váiəlèit] *v.*

To **violate** a law, rule, or agreement means to **break** it.

→ *I was given a ticket because the policeman said I* ***violated*** *the speed limit.*

Exercise 1

Choose the one that is similar in meaning to the given word.

1. merchandise
a. stores b. money c. goods d. fame

2. corrupt
a. healthy b. bad c. angry d. nice

3. rubbish
a. trash b. power c. food d. truth

4. transaction
a. meeting b. friend c. test d. sale

5. revenue
a. concert b. guide c. income d. trade

6. manipulate
a. control b. explain c. decrease d. attempt

7. infrastructure
a. education b. science c. religion d. roads

8. headquarters
a. material b. base c. dream d. section

9. audit
a. enjoy b. leave c. inspect d. prepare

10. incentive
a. reason b. product c. waste d. idea

Exercise 2

Write C if the italicized word is used correctly. Write I if the word is used incorrectly.

1. ____ This is the *affluent* area of the city. It is where most of the poor people live.

2. ____ He added his trash to the large pile of *rubbish*.

3. ____ The company *automated* by hiring twenty new workers.

4. ____ This painting is an important part of the city's *infrastructure*.

5. ____ The *subsidy* helped the company recover some of the money it had lost.

6. ____ The store sold most of its *merchandise* in the sale over the weekend.

7. ____ The cook *violated* the two sauces together into one delicious sauce.

8. ____ She took the food out of the refrigerator and then *disposed* the door.

9. ____ The company's bank records were *audited*.

10. ____ Bigger kids sometimes find it easy to *manipulate* smaller children.

Exercise 3

Choose the one that is opposite in meaning to the given word.

1. violate
   a. borrow b. respect c. approve d. explain
2. affluent
   a. smart b. quick c. poor d. evil
3. dispose
   a. keep b. make c. feed d. speak
4. administrator
   a. singer b. student c. mother d. worker
5. legitimate
   a. free b. pretty c. wrong d. alert

Exercise 4

Write a word that is similar in meaning to the underlined part.

1. Getting to play with her friends was something to make her want to clean her room.
   ____
2. The act of selling something took place right before the shop closed.
   ____
3. By the end of the meeting, they had made into law the repair of the highways.
   ____
4. She illegally persuaded the guard, so he would let her into the secret meeting.
   ____
5. It was a good year for the banks, but it was a bad year for places that sell things to the public.
   ____
6. The person who controls the company is a very efficient manager.
   ____
7. The papers that she needed were at the building where the bosses worked.
   ____
8. The law-breaking company was stealing money from many of its investors.
   ____
9. Shawn is working for a law-following organization in a bad part of town.
   ____
10. The money made by our company was even better than last year's.
   ____

The Corrupt Administrator

Mr. Pig was an **administrator** at a big factory that made different kinds of **merchandise**. During a meeting at the company's **headquarters**, his bosses said they wanted the factory to make more money.

"If the factory makes more money, then you will too," his boss, Mr. Horse, told him. It was a great **incentive**. Pig had always wanted to be as **affluent** as his bosses.

Mr. Pig returned to the factory and started making changes. However, most were not very nice, and some were not **legitimate**.

First, he fired all his employees. Then he **automated** the entire factory. Machines now made everything, and the other animals, Mr. Rabbit, Mr. Sheep, and Mr. Dog had no jobs. Next, he **bribed** some **corrupt** senators into **legislating** special **subsidies** for the factory. Finally, instead of paying a company to **dispose** of the factory's **rubbish** properly, he **violated** the law by throwing it into the river to save money.

At first, all the changes to the factory's **infrastructure** created more **revenue**. But soon many stores could no longer sell the factory's goods at **retail**. It seemed that the machines couldn't make products as well as the workers. The customers were disappointed with the factory's merchandise.

There were other problems, too. The animals had told their friends and family to stop buying the factory's goods. Officials discovered the factory's rubbish in the river, and when they **audited** the company, they discovered that Pig had **manipulated** the law in order to get more money.

All **transactions** with Pig's factory stopped. The factory lost money, and Pig lost his job. He realized his mistakes too late. He had tried to become rich by saving money any way possible, but the cheapest way was not always the best.

Reading Comprehension

PART A Mark each statement T for true or F for false. Rewrite the false statements to make them true.

1. ____ Mr. Rabbit was an administrator at a big factory that made different kinds of merchandise.

____

2. ____ Some of the changes made to the factory were legitimate.

____

3. ____ Mr. Pig bribed some corrupt senators into legislating special subsidies for his factory.

____

4. ____ Mr. Pig violated the law by disposing of the factory's rubbish in the ocean.

____

5. ____ At first, changes to the factory's infrastructure created less revenue.

____

PART B Answer the questions.

1. During their meeting at headquarters, what incentive did Mr. Pig's affluent boss give him?

____

____

2. What happened to the other animals after Pig automated his factory?

____

____

3. According to the officials who audited Pig's factory, why did he manipulate the law?

____

____

4. What happened to Mr. Pig and his factory when all transactions stopped?

____

____

5. Why could the stores no longer sell goods at retail?

____

____

UNIT 5

Word List

assess [əsés] *v.*

To **assess** something means to judge the structure, purpose, or quality of it.
→ *She* ***assessed*** *the condition of the toy car before buying it.*

astonish [əstániʃ] *v.*

To **astonish** someone means to greatly surprise them.
→ *The amount of people that came to her party* ***astonished*** *her.*

commence [kəméns] *v.*

To **commence** something means to begin it.
→ *His speech* ***commenced*** *with a "thank you" to all who had helped him succeed.*

essence [ésəns] *n.*

The **essence** of something is its important qualities or basic characteristics.
→ *The* ***essence*** *of the argument was that both sides felt they had lost money.*

extract [ikstrǽkt] *v.*

To **extract** something means to remove it.
→ *The dentist* ***extracted*** *the woman's damaged tooth and put in a fake one.*

fabulous [fǽbjələs] *adj.*

If something is **fabulous,** it is extremely good.
→ *This strawberry is the best I've ever had. It's* ***fabulous.***

haste [heist] *n.*

Haste is speed in movement or action.
→ *In order to get to the meeting in time, he proceeds with* ***haste.***

impulse [impʌls] *n.*

An **impulse** is a sudden thoughtless urge to do something.
→ *Because of the scary noise, she had an* ***impulse*** *to run somewhere and hide.*

latter [lǽtə:r] *adj.*

Latter describes something last in a series or the second choice of two things.
→ *In the* ***latter*** *minutes of the game, the visitors scored the winning goal.*

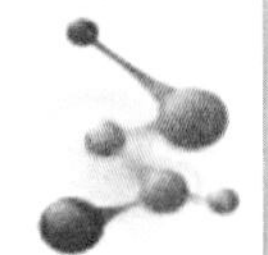

molecule [máləkjù:l] *n.*

A **molecule** is the smallest basic unit that makes up a physical substance.
→ *A tiny drop of water is made up of thousands of* ***molecules*** *of water.*

ongoing [ángòuiŋ] *adj.*

If something is **ongoing**, then it is still happening or still growing.

→ *The development of plants is **ongoing** because it takes time for them to mature.*

pharmaceutical [fà:rməsú:tikəl] *adj.*

If something is **pharmaceutical**, then it is related to the development of drugs.

→ ***Pharmaceutical** companies discover new cures to illnesses all the time.*

precise [prisáis] *adj.*

If someone is **precise**, then they are exact and careful about their work.

→ *The builder was very **precise** about where he placed the nails.*

proximity [prɑksíməti] *n.*

Proximity is closeness in time, space, or relationships.

→ *All the trees in the **proximity** of the beach had been cut down.*

publicity [pʌblísəti] *n.*

Publicity is public attention given to someone or something by the media.

→ *She received a lot of **publicity** after her performance in the film.*

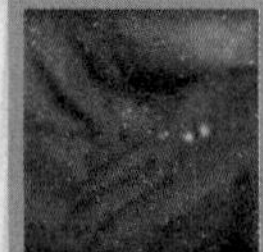

remedy [rémədi] *n.*

A **remedy** is a cure for a disease, argument, or problem.

→ *A good **remedy** for a headache is an aspirin and a glass of water.*

significance [signífikəns] *n.*

The **significance** of something is the quality that makes it important.

→ *The **significance** of the snowy weather was that we didn't have to go to school.*

subsequent [sʌ́bsikwənt] *adj.*

If something is **subsequent**, then it comes after something else in time.

→ *The flood and the **subsequent** rescue of those caught in the flood were on TV.*

synthetic [sinθétik] *adj.*

If something is **synthetic**, then it is made to be like something natural.

→ *Clothing made out of **synthetic** fabrics is very effective at keeping people warm.*

terminal [tə́:rmənəl] *adj.*

If something is **terminal**, then it causes or results in death.

→ *Since his condition was not **terminal**, he felt a great sense of relief.*

Exercise 1

Choose the one that is opposite in meaning to the given word.

1. remedy
   a. island b. instance c. movie d. poison
2. latter
   a. first b. rough c. temporary d. trivial
3. terminal
   a. brief b. chilly c. pleasant d. curable
4. commence
   a. rescue b. finish c. require d. twirl
5. precise
   a. moist b. insane c. messy d. hungry
6. synthetic
   a. natural b. rhythmic c. shiny d. harmless
7. extract
   a. manage b. anger c. insert d. explode
8. publicity
   a. gravity b. privacy c. bravery d. energy
9. impulse
   a. truck b. music c. revenge d. plan
10. fabulous
    a. rude b. noisy c. fertile d. awful

Exercise 2

Fill in the blanks with the correct words from the word bank.

Word Bank

subsequent	fabulous	impulse	publicity	extract
astonished	assess	terminal	essence	ongoing

The patient's illness seemed like it might be 1______________.
To save him, doctors had to 2______________ the infected tissue.

On an 3______________ he kicked the wall and it revealed a secret pass.
It led to his 4______________ escape from the prison.

It was difficult to 5______________ in which direction the forest fire would go.
One reason was that anything could happen while the fire was 6______________.

The 7______________ of the mayor's speech was about building the new library.
The building would be a(n) 8______________ addition to the scenery downtown.

His amazing skills during the last half of the game 9______________ the crowd.
Then that night, he received a lot of 10______________ from all the news shows.

Exercise 3

Write a word that is similar in meaning to the underlined part.

1. Because she took the test with such speed, she made several silly mistakes.

   ____

2. Her anniversary had a quality that made it important because it was also her birthday.

   ____

3. Though the smallest basic units in ice and steam are similar, their shapes are different.

   ____

4. They began the ceremony at 9:00 in the evening.

   ____

5. The closeness in space of her office is only a short distance from mine.

   ____

6. He could sleep late that day or get up early and start his work. He chose the second choice.

   ____

7. The noises on the computer sounded like they were made to sound like real ones.

   ____

8. Please judge the quality of his proposal before we decide to meet with him.

   ____

9. The best cure for a slightly injured foot is putting ice on it.

   ____

10. Most of the advertisements on TV are related to the development of drugs commercials.

    ____

A Famous Accident

One of the greatest **pharmaceutical** discoveries happened by accident. In his **haste** to go on vacation, Alexander Fleming had left his laboratory in a mess. The **essence** of his **ongoing** work involved a type of bacteria. An infection caused by the bacteria was often **terminal**, and he was looking for a **remedy**. He had left the bacteria out while he was away.

When he returned from vacation, he found that his lab was covered in fungus. He started cleaning up the mess. While he was cleaning, he had an **impulse** to examine the fungus. He saw that whenever the fungus was in close **proximity** to the bacteria, the bacteria died.

Though he was a messy scientist, his experiments were **precise**. He thought that there might be some **significance** to the fungus. He immediately **commenced** an experiment to **assess** what had happened to the bacteria. It had either died by accident or the fungus had killed it. The **subsequent** tests proved it was the **latter** reason.

What he found **astonished** him. The fungus actually killed the bad bacteria. All this time, he had been looking for a **synthetic** material to kill the bacteria. Instead, a common fungus did the job.

He knew that something in the fungus had killed the bacteria. His next step was to find those **molecules** that had done it. When he found them, he **extracted** them and put them into a pill. The drug proved to be very effective. It also worked against other types of harmful bacteria.

The discovery received a lot of **publicity**. Soon after, the new drug was being used all over the world. Because of the success, the scientist was able to develop even more **fabulous** drugs to help people. His accidental discovery changed the world and helped save many people's lives.

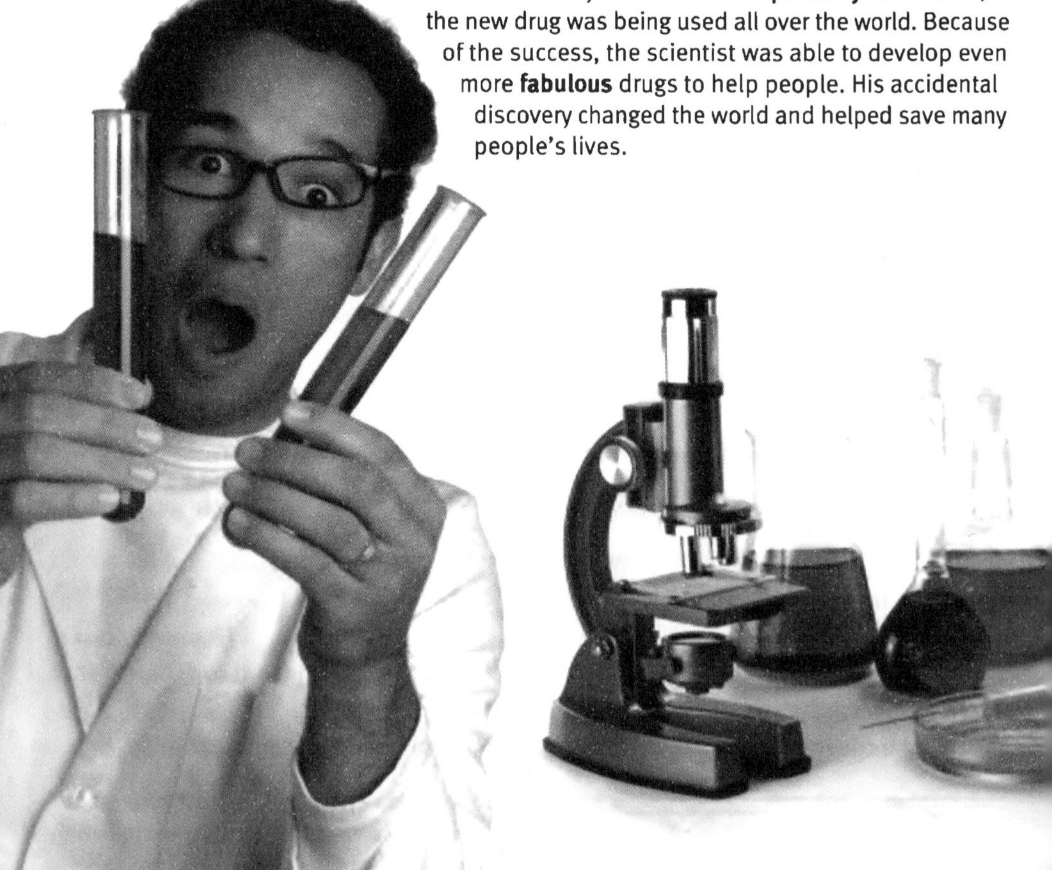

Reading Comprehension

PART A Mark each statement T for true or F for false. Rewrite the false statements to make them true.

1. ____ One of the most fabulous pharmaceutical discoveries was an accident.

   ____

2. ____ The essence of the scientist's ongoing work was to find a remedy for a terminal infection.

   ____

3. ____ The infection caused by the bacteria he was working on was not terminal.

   ____

4. ____ Fleming examined the fungus on an impulse.

   ____

5. ____ Whenever the synthetic material was far from the bacteria, the bacteria died.

   ____

PART B Answer the questions.

1. In his haste to go on vacation, how had Alexander Fleming left his laboratory?

   ____

   ____

2. What was the significance of the fungus?

   ____

   ____

3. When did the scientist get an impulse to examine the fungus?

   ____

   ____

4. What did the scientist extract molecules from?

   ____

   ____

5. What received a lot of publicity?

   ____

   ____

UNIT 6

Word List

altitude [æltətjuːd] *n.*

The **altitude** of a place is its height above sea level.

→ *The air was thin at such a high **altitude** on the mountain.*

coastline [kóustlain] *n.*

A **coastline** is the outline of a country's coast.

→ *He noticed that most of the cities in Australia are on the **coastline**.*

deter [ditəːr] *v.*

To **deter** means to prevent or discourage someone from doing something.

→ *Icy roads **deter** people from driving their cars.*

devise [diváiz] *v.*

To **devise** something means to have an idea or plan about it in the mind.

→ *The thieves **devised** a plan to steal the diamonds.*

expertise [ekspəːrtíːz] *n.*

Expertise is the knowledge and skills to do something well.

→ *John has a lot of advertising **expertise**. He can sell anything!*

fracture [frǽktʃəːr] *n.*

A **fracture** is a crack or break in something.

→ *Don't stand on that leg because there is a **fracture**. It might get worse.*

impair [impɛər] *v.*

To **impair** something means to damage it or make it worse.

→ *Drinking coffee **impairs** my ability to go to sleep.*

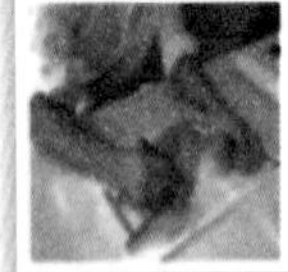

implement [impləmènt] *v.*

To **implement** something means to ensure that what has been planned is done

→ *The school decided to **implement** a new teaching strategy.*

indigenous [indidʒənəs] *adj.*

If something is **indigenous**, it is originally from, or native to, a place.

→ *Tomatoes are **indigenous** to the Americas.*

insight [insàit] *n.*

Insight is a deep and accurate understanding of something.

→ *The physics textbook gave the student new **insight** about gravity.*

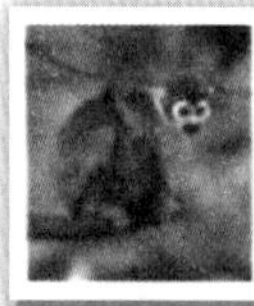

limb [lim] *n.*

A **limb** is a large branch on a tree.

→ *The monkey sat on the tree **limb** and enjoyed a piece of fruit.*

migraine [máigrein] *n.*

A **migraine** is a painful headache that makes one feel sick.

→ *My sister gets a **migraine** every time she has a lot of stress.*

optimism [áptəmizəm] *n.*

Optimism is the feeling of being hopeful about the future or success of something.

→ *The mother had **optimism** about her children's futures.*

peculiar [pikjú:ljər] *adj.*

When something is **peculiar**, it is strange, sometimes in a bad way.

→ *That **peculiar** smell coming from the kitchen reminds me of rotten eggs.*

proficient [prəfíʃənt] *adj.*

When a person is **proficient** at something, they can do it well.

→ *Secretaries are **proficient** at typing quickly.*

quest [kwest] *n.*

A **quest** is a long and difficult search for something.

→ *The treasure hunter went on a **quest** to find an ancient gold necklace.*

ridge [ridʒ] *n.*

A **ridge** is a long, narrow piece of raised land.

→ *The brown bear walked along the edge of the mountain **ridge**.*

spouse [spaus] *n.*

A **spouse** is the person to whom someone is married.

→ *I live in a home with my **spouse** and our two children.*

thrust [θrʌst] *v.*

To **thrust** means to push or move something quickly with a lot of force.

→ *The boxer **thrust** his fist into the punching bag.*

tolerate [tálərèit] *v.*

To **tolerate** something means to be able to accept it even when it is unpleasant.

→ *When you are in a hurry, it can be hard to **tolerate** traffic signals.*

Exercise 1

Choose the answer that best fits the question.

1. What would be hard to tolerate?
   a. A nice summer day b. A good movie c. A tasty dinner d. A broken leg
2. What is something that could be implemented?
   a. A plan b. A cloud c. A school d. A storm
3. What has a ridge?
   a. A person b. A mountain c. A swamp d. Fog
4. What would be peculiar to find in the ocean?
   a. A ship b. A shark c. A camel d. A piece of coral
5. What would impair vision?
   a. An eye test b. Rough fabric c. A strong smell d. A bright light

Exercise 2

Choose the one that is similar in meaning to the given word.

1. fracture
   a. a failure b. a break c. an idea d. a creation
2. limb
   a. a party b. an activity c. a branch d. a belief
3. thrust
   a. to push b. to grow c. to succeed d. to fall
4. indigenous
   a. rude b. extreme c. native d. cheap
5. devise
   a. to impress b. beautiful c. to plan d. confusing
6. optimism
   a. a good feeling b. to love c. to determine d. to reveal
7. insight
   a. a skill b. a journey c. a method d. an understanding
8. altitude
   a. layer b. height c. station d. freedom
9. migraine
   a. a headache b. a vehicle c. a chore d. a benefit
10. quest
    a. a problem b. a search c. a hero d. a story

Exercise 3

Write C if the italicized word is used correctly. Write I if the word is used incorrectly.

1. ____ The little girl loves her cat. She *tolerates* it when they are together.
2. ____ Going away to college is scary, but I have *optimism* that I'll have a good time.
3. ____ This *migraine* is killing me. My head hurts so badly that I can't think straight.
4. ____ My bike's tire is flat again. I guess I'll have to *impair* it.
5. ____ Her child is *peculiar*. He likes to wear his shoes on the wrong feet.
6. ____ The tree is getting too big for our yard! Ask Jim to cut off some of the *limbs*.
7. ____ I fell off my bike, but I didn't break any bones. I just got a slight *fracture* on my toe.
8. ____ This bush in my yard comes from another country. It's *indigenous* to my yard.
9. ____ From the mountain *ridge*, you can see the entire city below.
10. ____ Mike is a very *proficient* reader. He finished the entire novel in just an hour.
11. ____ We were in awe of the professor's *expertise* on the subject.
12. ____ You should *thrust* the baby when putting him in bed, so he doesn't wake up.
13. ____ I will get married to my *spouse* one year from today.
14. ____ Australia has a very long *coastline*.
15. ____ She is on a *quest* to find her long lost brother.
16. ____ If you don't like your job, you should *devise* it.
17. ____ She will have to get more *altitude* if she wants to swim faster.
18. ____ The workers *implemented* a new strategy to be more efficient.
19. ____ Nothing will *deter* me in my hunt for the perfect flower.
20. ____ Her *insight* into our problem really helped us out.

The Island

"Where am I?" Bob thought to himself when he woke up on a **peculiar** beach. "I can't remember what happened." There had been a bad storm, and Bob's fishing boat sunk. He washed ashore on a small island, but he had gotten hurt during the storm. He had a terrible **migraine**, and he had a **fracture** in his shoulder. He felt awful. But he had a strong desire to make it home to his **spouse** and children. He had to **tolerate** all the pain and **devise** a plan.

Bob stood up and looked around. "I'll walk to a higher **altitude**, so I can see everything around me," thought Bob. "Maybe I'll gain some **insight** about this island and find something to help me escape." As he walked along a mountain **ridge**, he noticed that the tall **indigenous** trees looked sturdy and thick. Bob got a brilliant idea. He could build a raft! He cut down some leaves and tree **limbs**. Even though his shoulder injury **impaired** his ability to carry the materials, he slowly dragged them down the mountain until he reached the **coastline**.

Bob was a **proficient** builder. He used his building **expertise** to line up the limbs and tie them together with long vines. When the raft was finished, Bob was happy with his work. "This will bring me home to my family," he said with a smile.

At last, Bob was ready to **implement** his escape plan. With all his might, he **thrust** the raft into the water. He climbed on and began the **quest** to find his way home. Bob smiled again, and thought, "I'm glad I kept a good attitude. It prevented the pain from **deterring** me from my plan. **Optimism** and ambition make anything possible." Slowly, he floated out to sea. In a few days, he made it to shore and ran home to see his happy family.

Reading Comprehension

PART A Mark each statement T for true or F for false. Rewrite the false statements to make them true.

1. ____ Bob had a migraine and a shoulder fracture when he awoke on the peculiar beach.

   ____

2. ____ Bob implemented a plan to bring his spouse and children to the island.

   ____

3. ____ The indigenous tree limbs impaired Bob's ability to carry the materials.

   ____

4. ____ Bob was proficient in building, and he used his expertise to build the raft.

   ____

5. ____ Bob thrust the raft into the water to begin his quest.

   ____

PART B Answer the questions.

1. What type of insight did Bob hope to gain when he moved to a higher altitude?

   ____

   ____

2. Why did Bob need to tolerate the pain and devise a plan?

   ____

   ____

3. What did Bob drag from the ridge to the coastline?

   ____

   ____

4. How did Bob prevent pain from deterring him?

   ____

   ____

5. What does Bob believe about optimism and ambition?

   ____

   ____

UNIT 7

Word List

aquatic [ǽkwətik] *adj.*

If a plant or animal is **aquatic,** it lives or grows in water.

→ *The dolphin is an **aquatic** mammal.*

biosphere [báiəsfìər] *n.*

The **biosphere** is the earth's surface and atmosphere where there are living things.

→ *Birds, trees, and worms all thrive in the **biosphere**.*

bizarre [bizάːr] *adj.*

When something is **bizarre,** it is very strange.

→ *My **bizarre** dreams make no sense to me when I am awake.*

Celsius [sélsiəs] *n.*

Celsius is a scale for measuring temperature.

→ *Water freezes at zero degrees **Celsius**.*

coarse [kɔːrs] *adj.*

If something is **coarse,** that means it has a rough texture.

→ *The **coarse** sweater made my skin itch.*

companion [kəmpǽnjən] *n.*

A **companion** is a person that someone spends a lot of time with.

→ *I always walk to school with my **companion** Frank.*

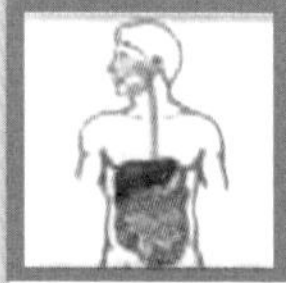

digest [didʒést] *v.*

To **digest** means to swallow food and pass it through the body.

→ *Allow some time for food to be **digested** before going swimming.*

duration [djuəréiʃən] *n.*

The **duration** of an event is the time during which it happens.

→ *The girls watched television for the **duration** of the evening.*

ecology [iːkάlədʒi] *n.*

Ecology is the study of the environment and living things.

→ *We study **ecology** to learn how to help improve the Earth.*

feat [fiːt] *n.*

A **feat** is an impressive or difficult achievement or action.

→ *The elephant's standing up on one leg was a **feat**.*

infinite [ínfənit] *adj.*

If something is **infinite**, it has no limit or end.

→ *Many scientists believe that the universe is **infinite**.*

nucleus [njú:kliəs] *n.*

The **nucleus** is the central part of an atom or cell.

→ *The **nucleus** is made up of many tiny particles.*

parasite [pǽrəsàit] *n.*

A **parasite** is a tiny animal or plant that attaches to another animal to get food.

→ *The sick dog was covered in **parasites**.*

prominent [prámənənt] *adj.*

When something is **prominent**, it is important and well known.

→ *Queen Victoria was a **prominent** person in history.*

repetitive [ripétətiv] *adj.*

When something is **repetitive**, it is repeated many times and becomes boring.

→ *Working on an assembly line making cars every day is a **repetitive** job.*

reproductive [rì:prədʌ́ktiv] *adj.*

If something is **reproductive**, it has to do with a living thing producing young.

→ *The **reproductive** system of a plant is simple.*

temperate [témpərit] *adj.*

When a place is **temperate**, it never gets too hot or cold.

→ *In Peru, the weather is **temperate** and rarely gets too hot or cold.*

tolerance [tálərəns] *n.*

Tolerance is the ability to accept something painful or unpleasant.

→ *Boxers have a high **tolerance** for pain.*

undergo [ʌ̀ndərgóu] *v.*

To **undergo** an action means to have it happen to you.

→ *The cancer patient **undergoes** treatments twice a week.*

vulnerable [vʌ́lnərəbəl] *adj.*

When someone is **vulnerable**, they are weak and without protection.

→ *He felt very **vulnerable** when he was stranded in the desert.*

Exercise 1

Fill in the blanks with the correct words from the word bank.

Word Bank

temperate	companion	ecology	vulnerable	parasite
Celsius	aquatic	bizarre	biosphere	feat

The climate where I live is very 1______________.
It never drops below 10 degrees 2______________.

I learned about a tiny animal called a 3______________.
Some live on land, and others are 4______________.

The strange old man's behavior is quite 5______________.
The plastic chicken he takes with him everywhere is his only 6______________.

Jim loves every type of plant and animal in the 7______________.
Therefore, he is going to college to study 8______________.

Without his shield, the sword fighter was 9______________.
Defeating his enemy without protection was an amazing 10______________.

Exercise 2

Write a word that is similar in meaning to the underlined part.

1. Dogs do not have the ability to bear the pain to high pitched noises.

   ____

2. The boring and repeating sounds from a ticking clock can make some people annoyed.

   ____

3. My sister is a well-known and important musician.

   ____

4. I used my microscope to see the cell's central part.

   ____

5. The rough fur of the gorilla is a defining trait.

   ____

Exercise 3

Write C if the italicized word is used correctly. Write I if the word is used incorrectly.

1. ____ The *reproductive* process in rabbits explains how they hunt for food.

2. ____ In Biology class, we learned about the different parts of a cell's *nucleus*.

3. ____ It is hard for some people to remain silent for the *duration* of a long movie.

4. ____ I could listen to my favorite song all day. I have *tolerance* for great music.

5. ____ I will have to *undergo* through the tunnel to get home.

6. ____ This blanket is not very comfortable. It would be better if it was not so *coarse*.

7. ____ She has exactly twenty jelly beans, which is an *infinite* amount.

8. ____ The boy became a *prominent* figure in town after he saved the woman's life.

9. ____ Her new car is *bizarre*. It has five wheels and no doors!

10. ____ There is no life on Venus, so researchers study its *ecology* instead.

11. ____ The *vulnerable* lion roared and scared away the zebras.

12. ____ Fish must live in *aquatic* environments.

13. ____ The circus performers were capable of many wonderful *feats*.

14. ____ The *repetitive* sound of ocean waves helps me to fall asleep.

15. ____ The cake *digested* the delicious cookies.

16. ____ The *temperate* nights were almost too cold to bear.

17. ____ *Parasites* are independent forms of life.

18. ____ I don't want to go alone. I wish I had a *companion*.

19. ____ Will you please *Celsius* the temperature outside?

20. ____ The drawing of the earth showed the different elements of the *biosphere*.

Small World

Even though people can't see me, I'm an important part of Earth's **biosphere**. Scientists who study **ecology** know that I was the first life form on Earth. There is more of my kind than any other plant or animal in the world. Without me, other plants and animals would not even exist. I am a protist, and my tiny body is made up of one single cell.

In my small world, things can be absolutely **bizarre**. Unlike most **aquatic** plants and animals, I don't need a **temperate** climate. I have a very high **tolerance** for extreme conditions. Right now, I'm swimming around in a bucket of boiling water! The temperature is 150 degrees **Celsius**, but I feel comfortable. I have **coarse** hairs called *cilia* that help me swim around in here. I move my cilia in a **repetitive** motion for the **duration** of my swim. I cannot go very fast, though. It takes me about five minutes to swim a distance of just one millimeter!

When I get hungry, I look for tiny, **vulnerable parasites**. I swim up to one and swallow it whole. I **digest** things much like people do. I have an organ that works just like a human stomach. After I eat, I release nitrogen gas. Nitrogen is a **prominent** gas in the earth's atmosphere. Other plants and animals need my nitrogen to survive.

My **reproductive** ability is my most unique trait. I don't need a **companion** to mate with. Instead, I **undergo** a process called *fission*, where my own **nucleus** splits in half. An exact copy of my nucleus is made, which forms into another protist. It really is an impressive **feat**. I can create an **infinite** number of new protists all by myself!

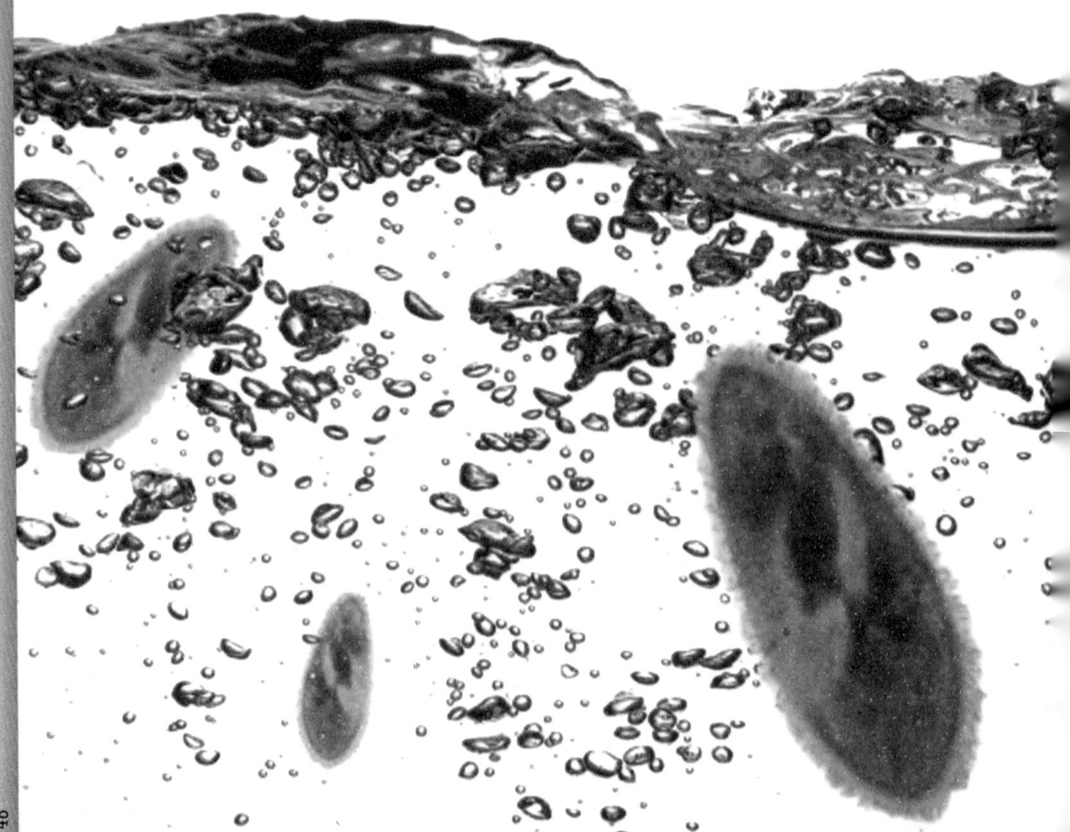

Reading Comprehension

PART A Mark each statement T for true or F for false. Rewrite the false statements to make them true.

1. ____ Protists have a high tolerance for temperate conditions.

____

2. ____ Things in an aquatic protist's world can be absolutely bizarre.

____

3. ____ A protist splits its companion's nucleus in fission.

____

4. ____ Coarse cilia move in a repetitive motion for the duration of a protist's swim.

____

5. ____ An infinite number of new protists can be created by the impressive feat of fission.

____

PART B Answer the questions.

1. What temperature, in degrees Celsius, could the protist be comfortable in?

____

____

2. What do scientists who study ecology know about protists?

____

____

3. What prominent thing does a protist release into the biosphere?

____

____

4. How does a protist catch vulnerable parasites to digest?

____

____

5. What unique reproductive process does a protist undergo?

____

____

UNIT 8

Word List

adept [ədépt] *adj.*

If someone is **adept** at something, they are very good at doing it.

→ *The carpenter is very **adept** at building houses.*

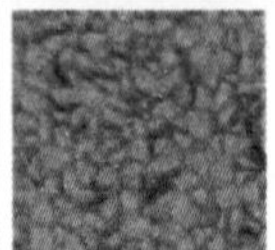

barren [bærən] *adj.*

If land is **barren,** it has no plants growing on it.

→ *People cannot farm in **barren** lands.*

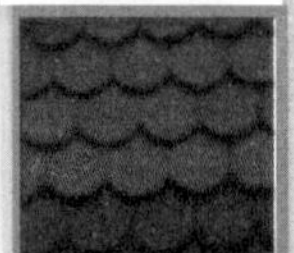

ceramic [səræmik] *adj.*

If something is **ceramic,** it is made of baked clay.

→ *The house's roof was made of **ceramic** tiles.*

culinary [kʌlənèri] *adj.*

If something is **culinary,** it is related to cooking.

→ *I gained **culinary** skills after working in a restaurant for many years.*

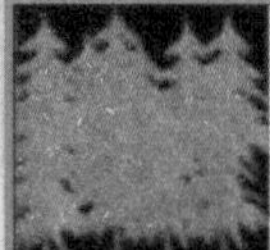

dense [dens] *adj.*

If something is **dense,** it has a lot of things close together.

→ *I easily became lost in the **dense** forest.*

dignity [dígnəti] *n.*

Dignity is the ability to be calm and worthy of respect.

→ *When his company went out of business, he faced it with **dignity**.*

dominate [dɑ́mənèit] *v.*

To **dominate** someone or something is to control them.

→ *The loud man **dominated** the conversation.*

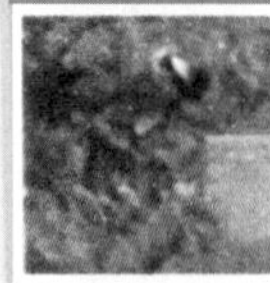

edible [édəbəl] *adj.*

If something is **edible,** you can eat it.

→ *We learn about **edible** plants when we go camping.*

hostile [hɑstíl] *adj.*

If someone is **hostile,** they are angry and unfriendly.

→ *We were happy to move away from our **hostile** neighbor.*

intake [íntèik] *n.*

Your **intake** of food is the amount of food you take into your body.

→ *The doctor said I needed to increase my **intake** of fruits and vegetables.*

likewise [laikwaiz] *adv.*

If someone does something **likewise**, they do the same thing as someone else.

→ *If Joe is staying away from school to go swimming, I want to do* ***likewise****.*

malnutrition [mælnju:triʃən] *n.*

Malnutrition is the condition of not getting enough nutrients.

→ *After eating only a meager amount of food, she suffered from* ***malnutrition****.*

medication [medəkeiʃən] *n.*

Medication is medicine or drugs given to people who are sick.

→ *The doctor gave me* ***medication*** *to treat my illness.*

misconception [miskənsépʃən] *n.*

A **misconception** is a wrong idea about something.

→ *People once believed the* ***misconception*** *that the Earth is flat.*

obscure [əbskjúər] *adj.*

If something is **obscure**, it is not well-known.

→ *The old man travels the world in search of* ***obscure*** *books.*

oppress [əpres] *v.*

To **oppress** someone means to rule over them in a cruel and unfair way.

→ *Free speech had been* ***oppressed*** *in his country.*

peel [pi:l] *v.*

To **peel** fruits and vegetables is to remove their skin.

→ *We* ***peeled*** *the apple before eating it.*

prescription [priskripʃən] *n.*

A **prescription** is permission from a doctor to get medicine.

→ *The doctor gave me a* ***prescription*** *for my medication.*

respirator [respəreitə:r] *n.*

A **respirator** is a machine that helps weak or sick people breathe.

→ *The man needed a* ***respirator*** *to breathe.*

strive [straiv] *v.*

To **strive** is to struggle to achieve something.

→ *People who* ***strive*** *to succeed often do.*

Exercise 1

Choose the answer that best fits the question.

1. If you need medication, you are probably _______.
   a. sick b. hungry
   c. bored d. skinny

2. If you have a misconception about something, _______.
   a. you are clear b. you are complicated
   c. you are wrong d. you are correct

3. Which of the following is true of a ceramic bowl?
   a. It is metal. b. It is clay.
   c. It is wooden. d. It is plastic.

4. If you are adept at painting, you can _______.
   a. paint badly b. paint like a child
   c. paint well d. only use certain colors

5. When you peel a piece of fruit, you _______.
   a. remove the skin b. cut it into pieces
   c. eat the skin d. take a knife and chop it up

Exercise 2

Fill in the blanks with the correct words from the word bank.

Word Bank

culinary	dominate	edible	hostile	intake
malnutrition	medication	misconception	peel	prescription

My boss is a difficult person to deal with because he can become so 1______________.
He gets incredibly angry when he can't 2______________ an employee or a customer.

There is a popular 3______________ that cooking well is difficult.
Actually, most people can cook with basic 4______________ techniques.

My 5______________ is about to run out, but I still need more.
Tomorrow, I will ask the doctor for a new 6______________.

The skin of some vegetables such as squash is not 7______________.
That is why you have to 8______________ it before you eat it.

In some parts of the world, 9______________ is a major problem.
One of the causes is inadequate 10______________ of necessary vitamins and minerals.

Exercise 3

Choose the one that is similar in meaning to the given word.

1. oppress
   a. cure b. print c. rule d. break
2. barren
   a. ugly b. mountainous c. close d. lifeless
3. strive
   a. attack b. struggle c. compete d. win
4. dominate
   a. control b. trick c. encourage d. entertain
5. culinary
   a. growing b. creating c. cooking d. drinking

Exercise 4

Write C if the italicized word is used correctly. Write I if the word is used incorrectly.

1. ____ One of my classmates is very *hostile*. He always helps me with homework.
2. ____ I chose an *obscure* book for my report. It was very difficult to find.
3. ____ In the past, many people suffered from *malnutrition* because of a lack of food.
4. ____ Did you know that some flowers are *edible*? They both look and taste good.
5. ____ The dog was hiding in a *dense* patch of grass. We had no trouble finding him.
6. ____ People enjoy Mark Twain's novels. They *likewise* enjoy his political comments.
7. ____ You can have health problems if your sugar *intake* is too high.
8. ____ You need to ask your teacher for a *prescription*. Then you can get your medicine.
9. ____ After we lost the game, our coach showed his *dignity*. He yelled at us for hours.
10. ____ After the car accident, John needed a *respirator*. He could not walk without it.
11. ____ They are taking a break outside. Why don't we do *likewise*?
12. ____ A month ago, I hurt myself playing soccer. The injury finally *oppressed* this week.
13. ____ *Strive* to do worst on your test.
14. ____ I *strive* to exercise at least twenty minutes each day to stay in shape.
15. ____ Many deserts are *barren* landscapes. You find little more than dirt and rocks there.

Becoming a Healer

Years ago, I worked at a small health clinic in a remote country. I had gone there to treat an **obscure** syndrome. It attacked people's lungs, causing them to need a **respirator** to breathe. I was trying out a new **medication** to treat these people instead of using a respirator. If I was successful, I would become famous.

Everything was going fine until war broke out in a nearby country. Many people from that country fled the **hostile** invading army. The army wanted to **dominate** the people, but the people didn't want to be **oppressed**. So they walked hundreds of miles across **barren** land to get away.

Some of these people came to our clinic for treatment. I talked with them and learned of their difficulties. They did not beg or complain. I was impressed by their **dignity**.

There was one woman I will never forget. Her son suffered from **malnutrition** and stomach pain, and she didn't know what to do. Neither did I. I was not **adept** at treating malnutrition. Nonetheless, when I saw her sadness, I knew I had to help her son.

The woman had been feeding her son bread and water. She had a **misconception** that it would be enough for him. However, I knew that he needed to eat vegetables, too. So I took her outside and showed her a **dense** patch of **edible** plants. I taught her how to dig up the roots, **peel** them, and cook them for her son. I explained that she should increase her son's **intake** of these vegetables. **Likewise**, she should **strive** to get him some meat once a week to help him regain his strength.

I sent her off with a **prescription** for some pain medicine, but she also left my office with some new **culinary** skills. A few weeks later, she returned to tell me her son was healthy again. As thanks, she gave me a beautiful **ceramic** bowl.

I never became famous, but I kept that bowl to remind me what it truly means to heal someone.

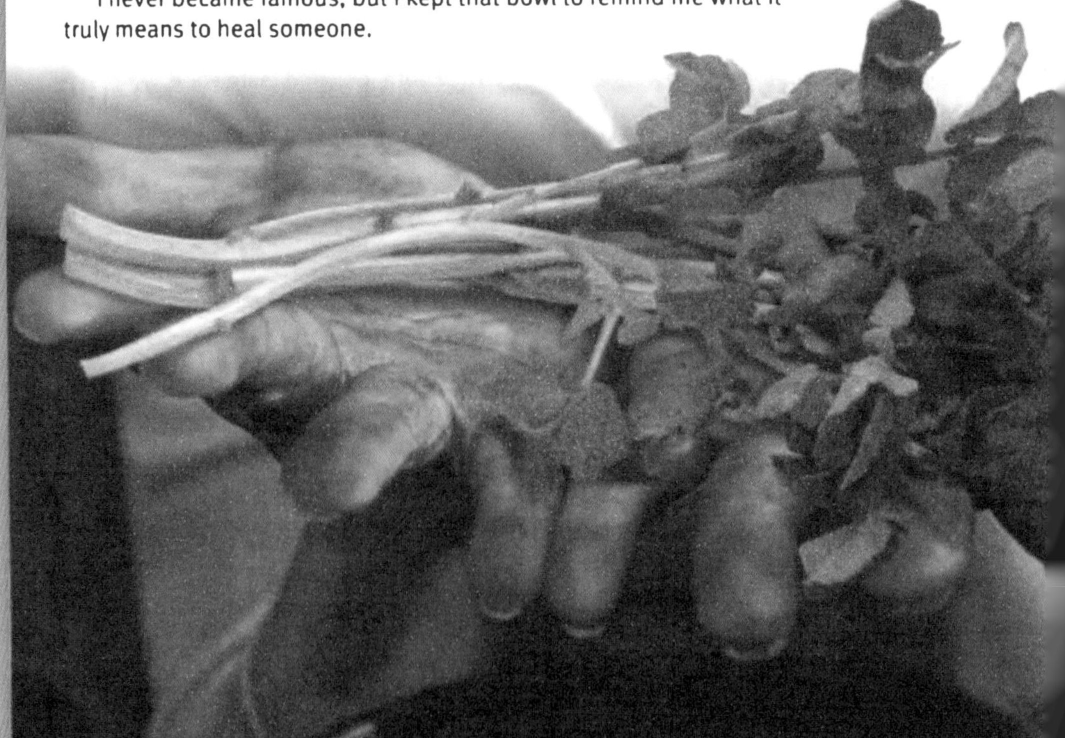

Reading Comprehension

PART A Mark each statement T for true or F for false. Rewrite the false statements to make them true.

1. ____ The respirator helped people with the obscure syndrome, and the doctor hoped the medication would do likewise.

____

2. ____ The hostile doctor wanted to dominate and oppress the people.

____

3. ____ The doctor was not adept at treating malnutrition before meeting the mother and her son.

____

4. ____ The doctor showed the woman a dense patch of barren land.

____

5. ____ The woman gave the doctor a ceramic bowl to show off her pottery skills.

____

PART B Answer the questions.

1. Instead of a respirator, what did the doctor use to treat the syndrome?

____

____

2. What misconception did the woman have about her son's food intake?

____

____

3. Why did the doctor teach the woman to peel and cook the roots?

____

____

4. What kind of prescription did the doctor give to the woman?

____

____

5. Why did the doctor ask the woman to strive to get meat for her son?

____

____

UNIT 9

Word List

archaic [ɑːrkéik] *adj.*

If something is **archaic**, it is very old or outdated.

→ *To be competitive, we must update our **archaic** equipment.*

benevolent [bənévələnt] *adj.*

If someone is **benevolent**, they are kind and generous.

→ *My father was a **benevolent** man and gave lots of money to charity.*

brass [bræs] *n.*

Brass is a metal that is used to make musical instruments and ornaments.

→ ***Brass** is used to make musical instruments like trumpets.*

capitalism [kǽpitəlizəm] *n.*

Capitalism is an economic system where private companies make goods for profit.

→ *Most industries in the world today are based on **capitalism**.*

component [kəmpóunənt] *n.*

A **component** is a part of a larger machine.

→ *Computers have many different **components**, so they are complicated to build.*

dependence [dipéndəns] *n.*

Dependence is a situation in which somebody relies on something else.

→ *Young children have a **dependence** on their parents.*

diminish [dəminiʃ] *v.*

To **diminish** means to reduce or get smaller.

→ *As the economy got worse, my savings **diminished**.*

drawback [drɔ́ːbæ̀k] *n.*

A **drawback** is a disadvantage.

→ *The **drawback** of having a car is that it is very expensive to maintain.*

fad [fæd] *n.*

A **fad** is something that is popular for a short time.

→ *The hula hoop was a **fad** for a few years, but it soon lost its popularity.*

impose [impóuz] *v.*

To **impose** means to interrupt or force your ideas on other people.

→ *He **imposes** on his wife every morning by expecting her to make breakfast.*

managerial [mæ̀nədʒíəriəl] *adj.*

Managerial describes something related to a manager or management.

→ *Nancy has a **managerial** position at the bank.*

medieval [mìːdiíːvəl] *adj.*

If something is **medieval,** it comes from the period between 650 and 1500 CE.

→ *We visited a castle that was built during **medieval** times.*

obsolete [ɑ̀bsəlíːt] *adj.*

If something is **obsolete,** it is not used anymore because something better exists.

→ *Since computers became inexpensive, typewriters have become **obsolete**.*

peninsula [pənínsələ] *n.*

A **peninsula** is a large piece of land that is surrounded by the sea on three sides.

→ *The state of Florida is an example of a **peninsula**.*

prestige [prestíːdʒ] *n.*

If a person has **prestige,** people admire or respect them.

→ *The young actress gained much **prestige** after she won an award.*

proportion [prəpɔ́ːrʃən] *n.*

A **proportion** is an amount that shows the link between the parts and the whole.

→ *Only a small **proportion** of the people in this town actually work here.*

radical [rǽdikəl] *adj.*

If something is **radical,** it is very new or different.

→ *The president is planning to make some **radical** changes to the law.*

refute [rifjúːt] *v.*

To **refute** something means to prove that it is false or incorrect.

→ *The bank manager has **refuted** the claims that he lied to his customers.*

spectacular [spektǽkjələr] *adj.*

If something is **spectacular,** it looks or sounds very impressive.

→ *There was a **spectacular** fireworks display in the park at New Year.*

weave [wiːv] *v.*

To **weave** means to make cloth using horizontal and vertical threads.

→ *We saw a woman **weave** a blanket on our vacation to South America.*

Exercise 1

Choose the answer that best fits the question.

1. What is something that is archaic?
   a. A computer b. An Egyptian pyramid c. Some bread d. Space ships
2. Which of these things is often made of brass?
   a. A saxophone b. A coat c. A chair d. A doll
3. Which of these is a component in a radio?
   a. Music b. Wires c. A television d. Diamonds
4. Which of these things could be seen during the medieval ages?
   a. Telephones b. Skateboards c. Castles d. Soda
5. If you are on a small peninsula, you will be quite near to ________.
   a. the mountains b. a forest c. the sea d. the moon

Exercise 2

Choose the one that is opposite in meaning to the given word.

1. weave
   a. to sew b. to create c. to pull apart d. to move
2. managerial
   a. entry-level b. legislative c. ruling d. supervisory
3. prestige
   a. fame b. honor c. sin d. lowliness
4. drawback
   a. artist b. benefit c. disadvantage d. boost
5. obsolete
   a. old b. innovative c. stale d. bright

Exercise 3

Choose the one that is similar in meaning to the given word.

1. benevolent
   a. crazy b. kind c. angry d. dark
2. diminish
   a. buy b. decide c. ignore d. decrease
3. radical
   a. new b. closure c. picture d. disadvantage
4. spectacular
   a. unusual b. sad c. amazing d. sudden
5. fad
   a. trend b. annoyance c. equipment d. sale

Exercise 3

Write C if the italicized word is used correctly. Write I if the word is used incorrectly.

1. ____ Knights in armor and their squires were common sites in *medieval* times.
2. ____ Our new boss hasn't made any changes to the company. He has very *radical* ideas.
3. ____ I don't want to *impose* on my father to help me with my homework. He's very busy.
4. ____ He *refuted* me because I didn't wash the plates after dinner.
5. ____ In *capitalism*, people can own just about any product or object they want.

Exercise 5

Write a word that is similar in meaning to the underlined part.

1. Our hotel was situated on a piece of land that was surrounded by the sea on three sides.

   ____

2. Doctors say the exercise can reduce the chances of getting ill.

   ____

3. Children's reliance on their parents decreases as they get older.

   ____

4. There are a number of disadvantages to taking up this new technology.

   ____

5. A large amount of students from my school want to go to university.

   ____

6. I need to buy some new parts for my computer to make it work properly.

   ____

7. I'm sorry to interrupt and intrude on you, but I need some help with my car.

   ____

8. The newspaper editor disproved the claim that the stories in the paper were untrue.

   ____

9. The show at the theater was very impressive.

   ____

10. The kind and generous women gave lots of money to help the poor.

    ____

The Weaving Machine

Mr. Joseph Franklin invented a machine that could **weave** cloth. It wove faster and straighter than anyone could weave by hand. He decided to take it to two cities on a **peninsula**, Netherton and Wilton. In these cities, a large **proportion** of the people worked in weaving. Joseph felt sure he could sell his machine there.

Joseph first took his machine to the mayor of Netherton. "Think of the money you will earn from this machine!" Joseph said to him.

But the mayor was a **benevolent** man. He knew about the people's **dependence** on weaving for their livelihood. If he bought the machine, the people would lose their jobs. So he refused to buy it.

Joseph said, "We are no longer in the **medieval** age! Soon everything will be made by machines. Cloth made by hand will soon be **obsolete**. If you don't change your **archaic** ways, your town's income will **diminish**!"

But the mayor said, "I don't like **capitalism**. Don't **impose** your **radical** ideas on my town. Go away!"

So Joseph took his machine to the mayor at Wilton. This mayor thought Joseph's machine was **spectacular** and spent a long time looking at its different **components** made of **brass**. The mayor couldn't **refute** the fact that the machine had **drawbacks** that would affect the people's jobs. But he realized the machine could bring money and **prestige**. So he ordered Joseph to build twenty of them.

Within a year, Wilton was a wealthy city, famous for its wonderful cloth. People no longer wove but worked in **managerial** jobs at cloth factories instead. Nobody bought the cloth from Netherton anymore. The people of Netherton became poor and hungry.

Finally, the mayor of Netherton called Joseph and said, "Now I realize that your machine is not just a passing **fad**. To succeed in business, we must be willing to change." He then ordered twenty weaving machines.

After that, both Netherton and Wilton became rich cities, famous throughout the land for their wonderful cloth.

Reading Comprehension

PART A Mark each statement T for true or F for false. Rewrite the false statements to make them true.

1. ____ The mayor of Netherton wanted Joseph to impose his radical fad on the town.

2. ____ Joseph thought the mayor of Netherton's ideas were medieval and archaic.

3. ____ The mayor of Wilton refuted the fact that the machine had drawbacks.

4. ____ In Wilton, the people who used to weave got managerial positions at the factories.

5. ____ In the end, capitalism brought prestige to both cities.

PART B Answer the questions.

1. What job did a large proportion of the people on the peninsula do?

2. According to Joseph, what will soon be obsolete?

3. What did the benevolent mayor of Netherton realize about the people's dependence on weaving?

4. What did the mayor of Wilton realize about the spectacular machine with components made of brass?

5. Why did income diminish in Netherton after machines were introduced in Wilton?

UNIT 10

Word List

accountant [əkáuntənt] *n.*

An **accountant** is a person whose job is to keep financial accounts.

→ *The **accountant** helped me keep track of my money.*

capitalist [kǽpitəlist] *n.*

A **capitalist** is a business person who invests in trade and industry for profit.

→ *The **capitalist** invested in a factory that made wheat into cereal.*

contempt [kəntémpt] *n.*

Contempt is the feeling of having no respect for something.

→ *The judge had **contempt** for the wicked criminal.*

dedicate [dédikèit] *v.*

To **dedicate** oneself to something means to put a lot of time and effort into it.

→ *The nun **dedicated** herself to helping people in need.*

ditch [ditʃ] *n.*

A **ditch** is a narrow hole cut into the ground by a road or a field.

→ *When the car slid off of the road, it fell into the **ditch**.*

enterprise [éntərpràiz] *n.*

An **enterprise** is a company or business.

→ *My father owns an advertising **enterprise**.*

exquisite [ikskwizit] *adj.*

When something is **exquisite,** it is very beautiful or pleasant.

→ *The artist made **exquisite** watercolor paintings.*

finance [finǽns] *v.*

To **finance** someone or something means to provide money for them.

→ *The government **financed** the scientist's experiments with new weapons.*

indifferent [indifərənt] *adj.*

When someone is **indifferent** toward something, they have a lack of interest in it.

→ *Lisa is **indifferent** toward school. She doesn't care what her final grades are.*

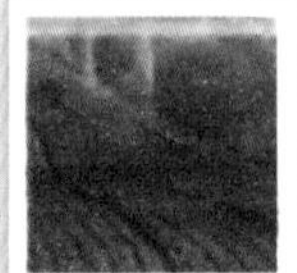

irrigate [írəgèit] *v.*

To **irrigate** means to supply water to land so that crops can grow.

→ *In dry climates, it is important to **irrigate** fields of crops.*

maximize [mǽksəmàiz] *v.*

To **maximize** something is to make it as great in amount, size, or importance.
→ *You should exercise regularly to* ***maximize*** *a healthy lifestyle.*

monetary [mánətèri] *adj.*

When something is **monetary**, it relates to money.
→ *A strong* ***monetary*** *policy is important for a country to be successful.*

precaution [prikɔ́:ʃən] *n.*

A **precaution** is an action that is meant to stop something bad from happening.
→ *As a* ***precaution,*** *you should put on a heavy coat before going out in cold weather.*

preliminary [prilímənéri] *adj.*

Preliminary describes something that happens before a more important event.
→ *The runners must do well in the* ***preliminary*** *races to qualify for the final race.*

saturate [sǽtʃərèit] *v.*

To **saturate** something means to completely soak it with a liquid.
→ *The sponge was* ***saturated*** *with soapy water and dripped all over the floor.*

simplicity [simplísəti] *n.*

The **simplicity** of something is the fact that it is easy to do or understand.
→ *We were able to find the house thanks to the* ***simplicity*** *of the directions.*

sow [sou] *v.*

To **sow** seeds means to plant them in the ground.
→ *He always* ***sows*** *his garden seeds in the springtime.*

soy [sɔi] *n.*

Soy is a food made from soybeans, such as flour or butter.
→ ***Soy*** *can be made into tofu, sauce, and also milk.*

spade [speid] *n.*

A **spade** is a tool used for digging.
→ *The gardener used her* ***spade*** *to make a hole for the seed.*

upcoming [ʌ́pkʌmiŋ] *adj.*

When something is **upcoming,** that means it will happen in the near future.
→ *The kids were worried about their* ***upcoming*** *exam.*

Exercise 1

Choose the answer that best fits the question.

1. What is a type of enterprise?
   a. A church b. A sign company c. A textbook d. A date
2. What kind of person would most people have contempt for?
   a. A killer b. A student c. A farmer d. A veterinarian
3. Which of these things would you most likely want to maximize?
   a. Your foolishness b. Your debt c. Your income d. Your weight
4. Where would you most likely find a ditch?
   a. By a road b. In a person's backyard c. In a tree d. In a classroom
5. What might a person sow?
   a. Apple seeds b. Dresses c. Animals d. Cake

Exercise 2

Choose the one that is similar in meaning to the given word.

1. maximize
   a. victory b. creation c. thought d. to make great
2. sow
   a. to plant b. to fail c. to climb d. to understand
3. upcoming
   a. slow b. soon c. uncommon d. ready
4. exquisite
   a. sure b. beautiful c. complete d. believable
5. enterprise
   a. a car b. a business c. an animal d. a group
6. ditch
   a. a ride b. a river c. a channel d. a home
7. contempt
   a. praise b. taste c. rating d. no respect
8. spade
   a. a fan b. a tool c. a trait d. a fact
9. irrigate
   a. to water b. to write c. to find d. to destroy
10. simplicity
    a. pride b. faith c. fondness d. easiness

Exercise 3

Write C if the italicized word is used correctly. Write I if the word is used incorrectly.

1. ____ I think the *soy* beans would taste better if we cooked them first.
2. ____ Jim said he would *finance* their new store for a share of their profits.
3. ____ We all knew the *precaution* of our actions would be terrible.
4. ____ The *preliminary* whistle blew, meaning the game was over.
5. ____ It can be difficult to keep track of *monetary* matters.
6. ____ The *indifferent* fan cheered loudly for his favorite team.
7. ____ The *capitalist* believed that his efforts would lead to great profits in the future.
8. ____ The company *accountant* found an error in the bank statement.
9. ____ I need to *dedicate* my house before the winter season.
10. ____ The rain *saturated* the ground so much that it was as dry as a stone.

Exercise 4

Write a word that is similar in meaning to the underlined part.

1. My favorite cake is made using flour from beans.

   ____

2. The driver kept both hands on the wheel as a way to prevent something bad.

   ____

3. People who keep financial accounts have many important duties in a business.

   ____

4. I wish I knew the money-related value of my gold collection.

   ____

5. The preparation duties before the concert included testing the microphones.

   ____

6. The spilled juice completely soaked the small rug on the kitchen floor.

   ____

7. Many wealthy companies provided money for the private school.

   ____

8. That business person owns companies in many countries around the world.

   ____

9. She is lacking interest about what movie we choose to watch.

   ____

10. I want to decide to put the time and effort of myself to saving kittens.

   ____

Life on the Farm

Bill was an excellent **capitalist**. He **financed** a large aviation **enterprise** that made a lot of money. He knew how to **maximize monetary** gains in every business deal he made. Bill had one big problem, though. He was unhappy all the time. Bill knew that he had to do something about it, or he would be depressed for the rest of his life.

One day, Bill was in his office when he heard a knock at the door. "Come in!" Bill said loudly.

His **accountant**, Jane, walked in. Jane said, "Sir, I haven't seen you smile in a year. What are you so sad about? Your company is doing very well."

Bill told her, "I'm **indifferent** about my company's success. I have **contempt** toward my job. I just want to do something I enjoy. I've always loved growing plants as a hobby. I'm going to quit my job and become a farmer!"

"You're crazy!" Jane said.

"I don't think so," Bill replied. "I want the **simplicity** of a life on a farm. I'm tired of all this stress. Farming will make me happy."

The very next day, Bill carried out the **preliminary** task of buying land and tools. Then he got to work. He **sowed** many types of seeds. He planted **soy**, cabbage, carrots, and onions.

"The **upcoming** summer is going to be very dry," thought Bill. "I need to **irrigate** my crops as a **precaution**, in case it doesn't rain enough."

He took his **spade** and dug a **ditch** down the middle of his farm. "Water from the stream will flow down the ditch and **saturate** the soil around every plant," Bill thought.

Bill **dedicated** himself to farming. After a year, his farm looked **exquisite**. Most importantly, Bill was happy. He finally had the life he always wanted.

Reading Comprehension

PART A Mark each statement T for true or F for false. Rewrite the false statements to make them true.

1. ____ Bill could maximize monetary gains in the aviation enterprise that he financed.

   ____

2. ____ Bill was indifferent about the farm's success.

   ____

3. ____ Bill irrigated his crops as a precaution for the upcoming rain in summer.

   ____

4. ____ Bill dug a ditch with a spade.

   ____

5. ____ Bill sowed seeds and saturated the soy and cabbage plants.

   ____

PART B Answer the questions.

1. What did the accountant say when Bill said he would stop being a capitalist and become a farmer?

   ____

   ____

2. What did Bill have contempt toward?

   ____

   ____

3. What was the result of Bill dedicating himself to his exquisite farm?

   ____

   ____

4. What preliminary task did Bill perform?

   ____

   ____

5. What simplicity was important for Bill to get rid of his stress?

   ____

   ____

UNIT 11

Word List

acute [əkjúːt] *adj.*

When a bad thing is **acute**, it is very severe and intense.

→ *When she fell out of the tree, the girl felt an **acute** pain in her arm.*

aggression [əgréʃən] *n.*

Aggression is behavior that is mean or violent to others.

→ *The problem was only made worse by Mark's **aggression**.*

banquet [bǽŋkwit] *n.*

A **banquet** is a grand formal dinner.

→ *Both families brought a lot of food for the wedding **banquet**.*

biography [baiάgrəfi] *n.*

A **biography** is an account of someone's life that is written by someone else.

→ *We read a **biography** about Charles Darwin in science class.*

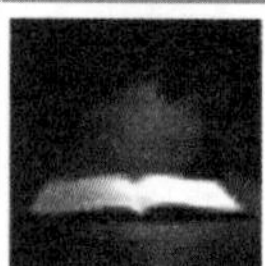

boost [buːst] *v.*

To **boost** something means to increase or improve it.

→ *Lowering prices **boosts** customers' interest in shopping.*

clap [klæp] *v.*

To **clap** means to hit one's hands together to express pleasure or get attention.

→ *After the speech, everyone in the crowd **clapped** their hands for the speaker.*

compel [kəmpél] *v.*

To **compel** someone to do something means to force them to do it.

→ *Traffic signs **compel** drivers to drive safely.*

dominance [dάmənəns] *n.*

The **dominance** of a person is their state of being more powerful than others.

→ *Large gorillas hit their chests to express their **dominance** over others.*

gorgeous [gɔ́ːrdʒəs] *adj.*

When something is **gorgeous**, it is very pleasing and attractive.

→ *The girl picked out a **gorgeous** dress to wear to the dance.*

inevitable [inévitəbəl] *adj.*

When something is **inevitable**, it is certain to happen or cannot be avoided.

→ *It is **inevitable** that the days will get longer in the summer.*

legacy [legəsi] *n.*

A **legacy** is an effect that exists because of a person or thing in the past.

→ *The **legacy** of the ancient Egyptians can be seen in their monuments.*

masterpiece [mæstərpi:s] *n.*

A **masterpiece** is a very good painting, novel, movie, or other work of art.

→ *The Arc de Triomphe is considered a **masterpiece** in the world of architecture.*

multiple [mʌ́ltəpəl] *adj.*

If there are **multiple** things, there are many of them.

→ *When the stunt went wrong, the man suffered **multiple** injuries.*

narrate [næreit] *v.*

To **narrate** a story means to write about it or read it aloud.

→ *This story was written by John, but Aaron is **narrating** it to the crowd.*

notorious [noutɔ:riəs] *adj.*

When something is **notorious**, it is well-known because of something bad.

→ *This area of town is **notorious** for gang activity.*

outdated [autdeitid] *adj.*

When something is **outdated**, it is old and no longer useful in modern time.

→ *Tape players are becoming **outdated** because of digital music.*

overall [ouvərɔ́:l] *adv.*

When a thing is talked about **overall**, the whole thing is considered.

→ ***Overall**, the party was a huge success.*

partiality [pɑ̀:rʃiæləti] *n.*

A **partiality** is a tendency to prefer one thing to another.

→ *She has a **partiality** for walking to school instead of driving.*

spontaneous [spɑntéiniəs] *adj.*

When an act is **spontaneous**, it is not planned. It happens suddenly.

→ *My wife made a **spontaneous** decision to buy a new sofa while I was at work.*

virtue [və:rtʃu:] *n.*

A **virtue** is a good quality or way of behaving.

→ *My best **virtue** is forgiveness.*

Exercise 1

Choose the one that is opposite in meaning to the given word.

1. gorgeous
   a. stiff b. unpleasant c. colorful d. cold
2. boost
   a. to lower b. to feel c. to increase d. to sleep
3. spontaneous
   a. short b. crowded c. planned d. faked
4. multiple
   a. one b. lousy c. grand d. free
5. inevitable
   a. heavy b. pretty c. silly d. avoidable

Exercise 2

Write a word that is similar in meaning to the underlined part.

1. I would like to write a <u>story about his life</u> for my father someday.

   ____

2. My little brother has an <u>awful, intense</u> case of chicken pox.

   ____

3. The entire family decided to talk to Father about his constant <u>violent behavior</u>.

   ____

4. The preacher strongly believed that kindness was the most important <u>good quality</u>.

   ____

5. The action in the play was <u>read aloud</u> by the teacher. The students read the rest.

   ____

6. The girl had a strong <u>preference over another flavor</u> for chocolate ice cream.

   ____

7. Black and white TVs are <u>no longer used in modern time</u> because people prefer color TVs.

   ____

8. The great actor left behind a great <u>result of his actions that continues to exist</u>.

   ____

9. She is <u>known for bad things</u> because she likes to hang around the wrong people.

   ____

10. I have no idea what would <u>force</u> Dan to act in such a mean way.

    ____

Exercise 3

Write C if the italicized word is used correctly. Write I if the word is used incorrectly.

1. ____ The good father was *notorious* for doing nice things for his family.
2. ____ We discussed the *overall* details of the plan.
3. ____ We planned our *spontaneous* vacation for weeks before we left for the trip.
4. ____ At the mayor's *banquet*, guests ate steak and lobster.
5. ____ It is polite to wait until the end of a play to *clap* for the performers.
6. ____ The *outdated* computer came with all the newest software.
7. ____ This novel is a *masterpiece* by the best writer of the 20th century.
8. ____ When the child got scared, he hid in the closet to show his *dominance*.
9. ____ A funny movie always *boosts* my mood when I am feeling sad.
10. ____ The sunset was so *gorgeous* that everyone turned away in disgust.
11. ____ The *acute* puppy rolled around on the floor.
12. ____ I moved to a different climate because of my *partiality* for warmer weather.
13. ____ I will write my own *biography* when I turn 50 years old.
14. ____ My need to pay rent *compelled* me to get a job and make enough money.
15. ____ Screaming loudly in the library is a *virtue*.
16. ____ One coat of paint was not enough, so I put on *multiple* coats.
17. ____ The author of this book *narrates* some famous battles.
18. ____ My *legacy* will be tested in the coming week.
19. ____ We knew a win was *inevitable* when our team was ahead by 100 points.
20. ____ I can be really mean. I wish I were better at controlling my *aggression*.

Beethoven's Gift

Beethoven was a great composer of classical music in the 1800s. Many **biographies** have been written that **narrate** his **dominance** in the music world. But do you know what really makes him special? Even though millions of people got to hear his **multiple masterpieces**, he never did. Beethoven wrote his best pieces after he went completely deaf!

His **partiality** toward classical music developed when he was very young. He wasn't interested in anything else as a child. When he was five, he learned how to play the piano. From then, nothing could stop his passion for writing and playing music.

When Beethoven was twenty, he began to lose his hearing. He got **acute, spontaneous** pains in his ears. His hearing kept getting worse over time. It was **inevitable** that he would eventually lose it altogether. It was very hard for him to keep writing music. He lost the **virtue** of patience, and he became **notorious** for his **aggression**. Still, he never stopped trying. His passion for music **compelled** him to keep performing even after he went deaf. He couldn't hear himself play, but he knew that his creations sounded **gorgeous**.

His final concert was held at a huge **banquet**. He gave the musicians a cue, and they began to play. He directed the concert with all his heart. He couldn't hear the music, but he said that he could feel it. **Overall**, performance was one of the finest in history. When it was over, he turned to the crowd. They **clapped** and cheered wildly. In that beautiful moment, the applause **boosted** his emotions, and he began to cry.

In 1827, he suffered from lead poisoning. He didn't survive the sickness, but his music did because great music never becomes **outdated**. Even though Beethoven is gone, his **legacy** will live on forever.

Reading Comprehension

PART A Mark each statement T for true or F for false. Rewrite the false statements to make them true.

1. _____ People have narrated biographies about Beethoven's dominance.

____

2. _____ Beethoven created multiple masterpieces that sounded gorgeous.

____

3. _____ It was inevitable that Beethoven would lose his virtue altogether.

____

4. _____ Beethoven became notorious for his aggression.

____

5. _____ Beethoven's legacy lives on because great music is outdated.

____

PART B Answer the questions.

1. What did the young Beethoven develop a partiality for?

____

____

2. How old was Beethoven when he first learned to play the piano?

____

____

3. What did Beethoven do when he saw the crowd clap and cheer at the banquet?

____

____

4. What compelled him to keep performing after his acute, spontaneous hearing loss?

____

____

5. What was special about Beethoven's last performance?

____

____

UNIT 12

Word List

anthropology [ænerəpɑ́lədʒi] *n.*

Anthropology is the study of people, society, and culture.

→ *In **anthropology** class, I learned about simple tools that ancient cultures used.*

applaud [əplɔ́:d] *v.*

To **applaud** means to clap in order to show approval.

→ *Everyone cheered and **applauded** Manny's efforts.*

appoint [əpɔ́int] *v.*

To **appoint** someone to a job means to give the job to them.

→ *Two students were **appointed** to help the scientists with their research.*

compatible [kəmpǽtəbəl] *adj.*

When things are **compatible**, they work well or exist together successfully.

→ *Jan and Fred are too different. They will never be **compatible**.*

competence [kɑ́mpətəns] *n.*

Competence is the ability to do something well or effectively.

→ *The job was easy because the group had enough **competence** to do it well.*

confer [kənfə́:r] *v.*

To **confer** with someone means to discuss something with them to make a decision.

→ *I will have to **confer** with my wife before I can purchase a new car.*

consecutive [kənsékjətiv] *adj.*

When things are **consecutive**, they happen one after another without interruption.

→ *The king ruled for ten **consecutive** years.*

crude [kru:d] *adj.*

When something is **crude**, it is not exact or detailed, but it can still be useful.

→ *She drew **crude** hearts on the ground to show how much she loved him.*

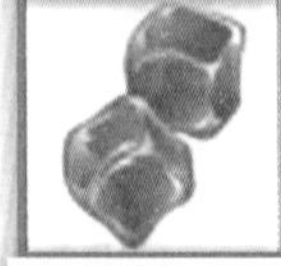

cube [kju:b] *n.*

A **cube** is a solid object with six square surfaces that are all the same size.

→ *Please get me some ice **cubes** to put in my soda.*

feedback [fí:dbæ̀k] *n.*

Feedback is comments to a person about how they are doing something.

→ *I asked my boss for **feedback** on my work.*

ignorance [ignərəns] *n.*

Ignorance of something is lack of knowledge about it.

→ *When he failed the test, his **ignorance** of math was obvious.*

masculine [mǽskjəlin] *adj.*

When something is **masculine**, it is a quality or thing related to men.

→ *American football is usually considered a **masculine** sport.*

monument [mάnjəmənt] *n.*

A **monument** is a structure that is built to remind people of a person or event.

→ *A large **monument** was built to honor the brave soldiers.*

muscular [mʌ́skjələːr] *adj.*

When someone is **muscular**, they are very fit and strong.

→ *He exercised regularly so that his body could become **muscular**.*

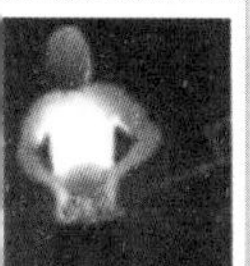

posture [pάstʃər] *n.*

A person's **posture** is the position in which they stand or sit.

→ *Your back will feel better if you improve your **posture**.*

situate [sítʃuèit] *v.*

To **situate** something means to place or build it in a certain place.

→ *The road was **situated** between the forest and the lake.*

supervise [súːpərvàiz] *v.*

To **supervise** something means to make sure that it is done correctly.

→ *Allen **supervised** the construction workers to ensure everyone's safety.*

symmetry [símətri] *n.*

Symmetry is the state of having two halves that are exactly the same.

→ *The artist made sure to use perfect **symmetry** when painting the butterfly.*

tattoo [tætúː] *n.*

A **tattoo** is a design that is drawn permanently on the skin with needles.

→ *The surfer had **tattoos** on both his arms.*

undergraduate [ʌ̀ndərgrǽdʒuit] *n.*

An **undergraduate** is a student at a college who is studying for a bachelor's degree.

→ *She was excited to finish high school and enroll as an **undergraduate** in the fall.*

Exercise 1

Choose the answer that best fits the question.

1. Which would need to be supervised?
   a. A car b. An experienced pilot c. A new student d. A boat
2. What is most likely something that is situated?
   a. A building b. An apology c. A disease d. A thought
3. What is something you can be appointed to?
   a. A television b. A job c. An illness d. A holiday
4. If someone confers with another person, ________.
   a. they fight b. they eat c. they discuss something d. they sleep
5. What is something that might be a cube?
   a. A box b. A shirt c. An airplane d. A disc

Exercise 2

Write a word that is similar in meaning to the underlined part.

1. I feel the best when the hours I sleep are <u>one after another without interruption</u>.

   ____

2. Even though he was young, the boy's facial features were <u>qualities related to men</u>.

   ____

3. My girlfriend and I are happy because we are <u>successful at existing together</u>.

   ____

4. The <u>strong and fit</u> fireman carried the children out of the burning building.

   ____

5. The <u>college student</u> handbook lists the classes I need to take to get my degree.

   ____

6. My mother was shocked when she found out I had a <u>permanent drawing on my skin</u>.

   ____

7. The first thing Al noticed about the new employee was his bad <u>standing position</u>.

   ____

8. This snowflake has perfect <u>halves that are the exact same but mirror images</u>.

   ____

9. He was embarrassed by his <u>lack of knowledge</u>.

   ____

10. The <u>not exact or detailed</u> measurements turned out to be good enough.

    ____

Exercise 3

Write C if the italicized word is used correctly. Write I if the word is used incorrectly.

1. _____ The *undergraduate* program at our school includes several possible degrees.

2. _____ She *conferred* with her coworkers before presenting their work to the boss.

3. _____ The rain made a *cube* on the grass.

4. _____ The *tattoo* appeared very dark on her light-colored skin.

5. _____ Our teacher was quick to give us *feedback* on our homework.

6. _____ The wall was *situated* in the north part of the yard.

7. _____ The baby *supervised* her mother in the store.

8. _____ The *symmetry* of the flower arrangement made it look very attractive.

9. _____ The angry father *applauded* his son when he got in trouble at school.

10. _____ The manager needed an assistant. She *appointed* Bill to the new position.

11. _____ The *masculine* girl looked very pretty in her new dress.

12. _____ In the final revision, he made sure his work was *crude*.

13. _____ The captain ordered the sailor to have better *posture*.

14. _____ The *muscular* movie star always got the role of the superhero in the movie.

15. _____ On our trip, we visited the *monument* built for George Washington.

16. _____ His *ignorance* led him to the final round of the tournament.

17. _____ My favorite subject in college was *anthropology*.

18. _____ She leaves the lights on at night because of her *competence* for the dark.

19. _____ When the couple got divorced, it was clear that they were *compatible*.

20. _____ Our basketball team won the championship for three *consecutive* years.

Brothers

John and Mark were brothers, but they were quite different people. Mark looked very **masculine**. He had a mustache and was very **muscular**. He was a sculptor. He made things out of stone. Mark was a good artist, but he was not very intelligent.

John looked nothing like his brother. He was small and weak, but he was very smart. John was an **undergraduate** in college, and he studied **anthropology** and history. He knew a lot about ancient cultures. The brothers loved each other very much, but they thought they had nothing in common.

One day, the mayor **appointed** Mark to build a **monument**: a statue of Egyptian Pharaoh, Tut. Mark agreed to do the job, but he had a problem. He had no idea who Pharaoh Tut was! However, he thought he had the **competence** to build a good statue anyway. He made some **crude** measurements and sculpted a statue of a very old man with a **tattoo** on his chest. Mark was proud of his work, but when John saw the statue, he laughed aloud.

"What's so funny?" Mark asked.

John replied, "Your **ignorance** makes me laugh. Don't you know that Tut was only a teenager when he was pharaoh? Let me help you. I'll **supervise** your work. I'll give you **feedback**, and we'll make this a great monument."

Mark got another **cube** of stone. John told him what Tut looked like. "Make him tall with good **posture**," John said. "And make sure there is **symmetry** in his body."

Mark **conferred** with John about every detail. For ten **consecutive** hours, the brothers worked. At last, the finished statue was **situated** in front of the museum. Everyone **applauded** the brothers' good work.

"We worked together very well. I guess we are **compatible** after all," Mark said.

John replied, "I agree! When we combine our talents, we are capable of greatness."

Reading Comprehension

PART A Mark each statement T for true or F for false. Rewrite the false statements to make them true.

1. ____ Mark's masculine features included a mustache and a muscular body.

   ____

2. ____ John laughed at Pharaoh Tut's ignorance.

   ____

3. ____ John appointed himself to supervise Mark's work and give him feedback about posture and symmetry.

   ____

4. ____ Mark made crude measurements and situated a tattoo on his original monument's chest.

   ____

5. ____ John was an undergraduate who studied sculpture and anthropology.

   ____

PART B Answer the questions.

1. Why did everyone applaud the brothers after ten consecutive hours?

   ____

   ____

2. What did Mark think he had the competence to do?

   ____

   ____

3. What did John explain to Mark after Mark got another cube of stone?

   ____

   ____

4. What did Mark confer with John about?

   ____

   ____

5. What did John say when he found out that he was compatible with his brother?

   ____

   ____

UNIT 13

Word List

brook [bruk] *n.*

A **brook** is a small stream.

→ *Water flows down several* ***brooks*** *on the mountain.*

cater [keitər] *v.*

To **cater** to someone means to provide them with all the things needed or wanted.

→ *Bill was too sick to get out of bed, so his nurse* ***catered*** *to his needs.*

considerate [kənsidərit] *adj.*

When someone is **considerate**, they pay attention to the needs of others.

→ *The* ***considerate*** *boy gave a present to his girlfriend on Valentine's Day.*

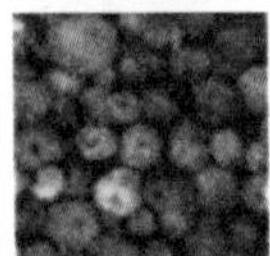

consumption [kənsʌmpʃən] *n.*

The **consumption** of food or drink is the act of eating or drinking it.

→ *These apples are too rotten for* ***consumption****.*

criteria [kraitiəriə] *n.*

Criteria are factors on which a person judges or decides something.

→ *Before she got the job, she had to meet all the necessary* ***criteria****.*

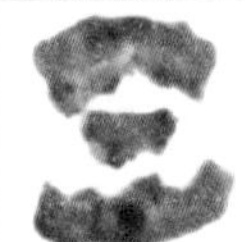

crust [krʌst] *n.*

Crust is the tough outer part of a loaf of bread.

→ *The little boy never ate the* ***crust*** *of his pizza.*

degrade [digreid] *v.*

To **degrade** someone means to cause people to have shame.

→ *The teacher* ***degraded*** *Bob when she announced his poor performance to the class.*

entitle [entáitl] *v.*

To **entitle** someone means to give them the rights to have or do something.

→ *His golden ticket* ***entitled*** *him to sit in the front row at the concert.*

escort [eskɔːrt] *v.*

To **escort** people means to safely accompany them to a place.

→ *Her bodyguards* ***escorted*** *her to the movie theater.*

external [ikstəːrnəl] *adj.*

When something is **external**, it is connected to an outer part.

→ *It is warm inside my house, but the* ***external*** *temperature is freezing.*

facility [fəsíləti] *n.*

A **facility** is a building that exists for a particular purpose.

→ *There are many educational **facilities** in big cities.*

faculty [fǽkəlti] *n.*

A **faculty** is a mental or physical ability.

→ *The boy's mental **faculties** impressed all of his teachers.*

heap [hi:p] *n.*

A **heap** of things is a large pile of them.

→ *After the building was torn down, all that was left was a **heap** of bricks.*

hemisphere [hémisfiər] *n.*

A **hemisphere** is one half of the earth.

→ *In the northern **hemisphere**, the weather is usually warmest in July and August.*

hound [haund] *n.*

A **hound** is a type of dog that is often used for racing or hunting.

→ *The men took their **hounds** with them when they went on the hunting trip.*

impersonal [impə́:rsənəl] *adj.*

If something is **impersonal**, it is not friendly and makes people feel unimportant.

→ *The boy felt scared on his first day at the big, **impersonal** high school.*

ornament [ɔ́:rnəmənt] *n.*

An **ornament** is an attractive object that people display in their homes.

→ *The woman kept some colorful **ornaments** on the shelves.*

pedestrian [pədéstriən] *n.*

A **pedestrian** is a person who is walking on a street.

→ *Cars should be careful when **pedestrians** are walking around.*

sanctuary [sǽŋktʃuèri] *n.*

A **sanctuary** is a place where people in danger can go to be safe.

→ *The church was made into a **sanctuary** for homeless people in the winter.*

spectator [spékteitə:r] *n.*

A **spectator** is someone who watches something, especially a sports event.

→ *There were thousands of **spectators** at the big game.*

Exercise 1

Choose the answer that best fits the question.

1. What is an external body part?
   a. A nose
   b. A heart
   c. A brain
   d. A skull

2. Which would NOT be considered a facility?
   a. A sports stadium
   b. A surfboard
   c. An auditorium
   d. A library

3. If you live in the southern hemisphere, you _______.
   a. are on the southern half of the earth
   b. are warm all-year round
   c. can't travel very far north
   d. are on your head

4. What does a pedestrian need the most?
   a. Good shoes
   b. A driver's license
   c. A bus pass
   d. Fuel

5. Which of the following is an example of crust?
   a. Hard cheese
   b. Outer part of a pizza
   c. A shell
   d. Pudding

Exercise 2

Fill in the blanks with the correct words from the word bank.

Word Bank

impersonal	hound	escort	spectators	considerate
faculty	pedestrians	brook	consumption	facility

You probably shouldn't take a drink from the 1______________.
The muddy water is not fit for 2______________.

When going to school, it is dangerous for small kids to be lone 3______________.
Parents should 4______________ them to school to ensure they arrive safely.

When I go hunting, I always bring my 5______________.
My dog has a great smelling ability. It's his best 6______________.

When we got to the stadium, I was amazed at the number of 7______________.
There must have been 50,000 people at the sports 8______________.

Because the dormitory was so big, I was afraid it would be 9______________.
But I was wrong. Everyone was very nice, helpful, and 10______________.

Exercise 3

Choose the one that is similar in meaning to the given word.

1. cater
   a. impressive b. to provide c. far away d. believable
2. degrade
   a. motherly b. likely c. ugly d. shame
3. heap
   a. a flash b. a jar c. a pile d. a pact
4. entitle
   a. to make happy b. to succeed c. to flee d. to give rights
5. criteria
   a. sadness b. letter c. market d. standard

Exercise 4

Write a word that is similar in meaning to the underlined part.

1. We went to the track to watch the racing dogs run.

   ____

2. The outer part of a loaf of bread was a dark brown and smelled like wheat and honey.

   ____

3. The baseball player was yelled at by an angry person who watches a sports event.

   ____

4. People who celebrate Christmas hang colorful attractive objects on their trees.

   ____

5. What are the factors on which you judge for becoming a member in your club?

   ____

6. The church was made into a place people can go to be safe after the hurricane.

   ____

7. Concentration is an important mental ability to have when studying for a test.

   ____

8. The messy girl kept her clothes in a pile on the floor.

   ____

9. The boy sat by the small stream and tossed stones into it.

   ____

10. Buying the house will give the rights to me to redecorate it any way I want.

   ____

The Old Hound

Elvis was a dog that loved to run. He possessed all the **criteria** to be a great racing dog. He had long legs, lean muscles, and a strong heart. He was so good that he never lost a race in the northern **hemisphere**. **Spectators** who bet on dog races always picked Elvis to win.

After ten years of racing, however, Elvis was getting old. His **faculties** were not as strong as they used to be. His owner got upset when Elvis started losing. Elvis's owner wasn't a **considerate** person. He **degraded** the dog all the time. Finally, his owner decided to get rid of him. He threw Elvis in his car and took him to the middle of the forest. He tossed him out and drove away. Elvis was cold and scared. He decided to follow a **brook** into the city.

Elvis soon found out that the city was a big and **impersonal** place. Everywhere he went, he saw signs that said, "No Dogs Allowed." **Pedestrians** yelled at him. He was sad, hungry, and alone. He thought that all people were as cruel and uncaring as his owner had been He was ready to give up when he heard a soft voice say, "What a beautiful **hound**!" Elvis looked up and saw an old woman. She said, "You're **entitled** to a better life than this. I can take you to a **sanctuary** for old dogs like you. I'll **cater** to all your needs. Would you like to come with me?"

The woman **escorted** Elvis to a beautiful **facility**. There was a sign on the **external** door that said, "Dogs Welcome!" The interior of the building was painted blue, and shiny **ornaments** hung from the ceiling. There was a **heap** of tasty bones and bread **crusts** for **consumption**. Elvis learned there were kind people in the world after all. He was so thankful that he jumped up and licked the woman's face.

Reading Comprehension

PART A Mark each statement T for true or F for false. Rewrite the false statements to make them true.

1. ____ Elvis possessed the criteria to be a spectator.

____

2. ____ Elvis's owner was not considerate, and he degraded the dog.

____

3. ____ Elvis followed the brook to the big, impersonal city where pedestrians yelled at him.

____

4. ____ In the interior of the facility, there was a heap of ornaments and bread crusts for consumption.

____

5. ____ The old woman wanted to cater to Elvis's needs at the sanctuary for old hounds.

____

PART B Answer the questions.

1. What was true of Elvis's faculties when he started getting old?

____

____

2. What did the old woman believe Elvis was entitled to?

____

____

3. What happened at all the races in the northern hemisphere?

____

____

4. Where was Elvis escorted to?

____

____

5. What was on the external door?

____

____

UNIT 14 Word List

asset [ǽset] *n.*

An **asset** is a skill or quality that is useful or valuable.
→ *The coach realized the boy's speed was an **asset** to the team.*

aspect [ǽspekt] *n.*

An **aspect** is one part or feature of something.
→ *I thought about the different **aspects** of owning two dogs.*

Braille [breil] *n.*

Braille is a system of raised patterns on paper that allows the blind to read.
→ *The boy enjoyed reading his favorite books written in **Braille**.*

bud [bʌd] *n.*

A **bud** is a part of a plant that turns into a flower or a leaf.
→ *Two weeks after planting the seed, a small **bud** appeared.*

coordinate [kouɔ́ːrdəneit] *v.*

To **coordinate** things is to make different parts work together.
→ *Each skating team had to **coordinate** their movements for the show.*

disprove [disprúːv] *v.*

To **disprove** something means to show that it is not true.
→ *The scientist **disproved** the theory that the sun moved around the Earth.*

humanitarian [hjuːmæ̀nətɛ́əriən] *adj.*

If something is **humanitarian,** it is connected to helping people's lives.
→ *After the flood, several **humanitarian** organizations offered help.*

hypothesis [haipɑ́θəsis] *n.*

A **hypothesis** is an idea for something that has not been proved yet.
→ *The teacher did an experiment to prove whether his **hypothesis** was right.*

imprint [ímprint] *n.*

An **imprint** is an effect or lesson from an experience that is hard to forget.
→ *The experience of war left an **imprint** on his mind that troubled him.*

informative [infɔ́ːrmətiv] *adj.*

When something is **informative,** it provides a lot of information.
→ *The travel guide had a lot of **informative** facts about the region.*

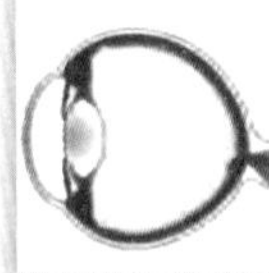

optic [áptik] *adj.*

When something is **optic,** it relates to the eyes or light.

→ *Her blindness was caused by a problem with her **optic** nerve.*

premise [prémis] *n.*

A **premise** is an idea on which something is based.

→ *The **premise** of the movie that Bobbi and I watched was unrealistic.*

rack [ræk] *n.*

A **rack** is an object with shelves that holds things.

→ *He stored his tools on a **rack**.*

Renaissance [rénəsɑ̀:ns] *n.*

The **Renaissance** was a period between the 14th and 17th centuries.

→ *Leonardo Da Vinci was a popular artist of the **Renaissance**.*

revere [riviə:r] *v.*

To **revere** something is to admire it greatly.

→ *The students **revere** their teacher, who has taught them a lot.*

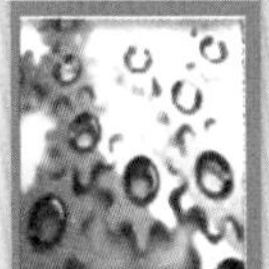

simultaneous [sàiməltéiniəs] *adj.*

When something is **simultaneous,** it occurs at the same time as something else.

→ *The movement of the gears inside the watch was **simultaneous**.*

skeptic [sképtik] *n.*

A **skeptic** is a person who does not believe something.

→ *The scientist showed the **skeptic** that dinosaurs did exist by providing evidence.*

spatial [spéiʃəl] *adj.*

When something is **spatial,** it relates to the position and size of things.

→ *He was asked where the books were located to test his **spatial** ability.*

specify [spésəfài] *v.*

To **specify** is to describe something clearly.

→ *The poster didn't **specify** where the concert was taking place.*

wax [wæks] *n.*

Wax is a substance that is slightly shiny and melts when heated.

→ *The candles are made of **wax**.*

Exercise 1

Choose the one that is similar in meaning to the given word.

1. informative
a. thoughtless b. careful c. helpful d. untrue

2. coordinate
a. to work together b. to break c. to listen d. to finish

3. premise
a. an important part b. a solution c. an idea d. a purpose

4. aspect
a. a valued thing b. a feature c. an idea d. a location

5. imprint
a. effect b. prison c. presence d. amount

6. rack
a. a baker b. a holder c. a shelter d. a waiter

7. optic
a. visual b. thoughtful c. medical d. restful

8. Braille
a. sign language b. hearing aid c. plant d. a system of writin

9. bud
a. tree b. sprout c. bark d. leaves

10. wax
a. bee substance b. light c. fire d. ice

Exercise 2

Choose the one that is opposite in meaning to the given word.

1. disprove
a. to invent b. to validate c. to lie d. to guess

2. revere
a. to disrespect b. to go fast c. to keep d. to put away

3. humanitarian
a. animal b. parasite c. assistant d. artist

4. simultaneous
a. frightening b. slow c. preceding d. lost

5. Renaissance
a. last b. modern c. art d. expensive

Exercise 3

Write C if the italicized word is used correctly. Write I if the word is used incorrectly.

1. ____ We received *humanitarian* relief after I got a terrible haircut.
2. ____ The boy waited for the *Renaissance*, which was going to start in the future.
3. ____ Alice placed the ball on the *rack* where all her sport equipment was stored.
4. ____ The woman liked the *premise* of the show, but she thought the acting was bad.
5. ____ The boy was scared by the *simultaneous* sound of the thunder and the phone.
6. ____ The map was *informative* and helped them from getting lost.
7. ____ The teacher *disproved* her expectations. He did exactly what she thought he would.
8. ____ Kelly had only met her uncle once and didn't know much about him. She *revered* him.
9. ____ In spring, all of the plants in the garden are covered with tiny *buds*.
10. ____ The *skeptic* didn't believe that the magician could actually make someone disappear.
11. ____ He didn't think about the *aspects* of smoking. Later he realized the disadvantages.
12. ____ The new hearing aid provides a wide range of *optic* choices.
13. ____ The bad dream left an *imprint* on Jared. He had forgot it by noon of the same day.
14. ____ He had to *specify* to the waiter whether he wanted onions in his food or not.
15. ____ The fruits looked real, but they were made of *wax*.
16. ____ Her understanding has been a real *asset* in her successful career.
17. ____ I did an experiment to prove my *hypotheses*.
18. ____ Please use the *spatial* spoon to turn the eggs.
19. ____ *Braille* has helped many blind people enjoy literature.
20. ____ If you *coordinate* all of sounds, you can make music.

Day Without Sight

On Friday afternoon, Sam's teacher had a special assignment.

"Next week, we'll be studying **humanitarian** efforts around the world since the time of the **Renaissance**, including those to help the blind," she said. "Over the weekend, I want each of you to wear a blindfold for an entire day. The **premise** of this experiment is that it will help you understand what it's like to be blind," she said.

Sam was a **skeptic**. He really didn't think the assignment would be too challenging. On Saturday morning, Sam took a piece of cloth and tied it around his head to cover his eyes. Then he went into the kitchen for breakfast. He heard the voices of his parents and brothers but couldn't **specify** where each voice was coming from. He thought about how important hearing is for blind people.

"Could you pass me the newspaper, please?" he asked. Just then, he remembered he couldn't see the words on the page. He wondered if **Braille** newspapers were ever made.

After finishing breakfast, his brothers asked him to play soccer. As he followed them, he accidentally walked into the baker's **rack**. He also found that he couldn't play soccer. He wouldn't be able to **coordinate** his actions without being able to see. Without his **optic** senses, he had no **spatial** awareness. Furthermore, he couldn't do **simultaneous** activities because he had to make sure he was safe first.

He sat on the lawn. Suddenly, he realized that though he couldn't see, his other senses worked perfectly fine. In fact, he began to realize new and different **aspects** of common objects. For example, he took a flower **bud** and felt it with his finger. He realized for the first time that it seemed to be covered with **wax**.

His **hypothesis** about being blind was **disproved**. The **informative** experiment had an **imprint** on him. It showed him sight was an **asset** that should be appreciated and taught him to **revere** the talents of blind people.

Reading Comprehension

PART A Mark each statement T for true or F for false. Rewrite the false statements to make them true.

1. ____ Sam's class is going to study humanitarian efforts since the time of the Renaissance next week.

 ____

2. ____ At first, Sam's hypothesis is that the assignment is going to be difficult.

 ____

3. ____ When Sam goes into the kitchen, he reads a Braille newspaper.

 ____

4. ____ Sam runs into the baker's rack on his way outside.

 ____

5. ____ Without his sense of sight, Sam has better spatial awareness and can coordinate his movements more easily.

 ____

PART B Answer the questions.

1. What was the premise of the experiment, according to Sam's teacher?

 ____

 ____

2. What did Sam realize when he couldn't specify where the voices were coming from?

 ____

 ____

3. Why wasn't Sam able to perform simultaneous activities?

 ____

 ____

4. What aspect of the flower bud did Sam notice after he realized all his other senses worked fine?

 ____

 ____

5. After Sam's theory was disproved, what was the impact the experiment had on him?

 ____

 ____

UNIT 15

Word List

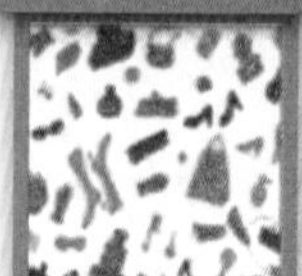

accessory [æksesəri] *n.*

An **accessory** is a thing that is added to another thing to make it look better.
→ *The store sold colorful **accessories** like bags, sunglasses, and makeup.*

acquisition [ækwəziʃən] *n.*

An **acquisition** is something that a person buys or gets in some way.
→ *Marty was happy with his new **acquisition**: a very fast bicycle.*

adequate [ædikwit] *adj.*

When something is **adequate**, it is good enough for something else.
→ *Without **adequate** notice of the road block, they will have to turn around.*

cardboard [ká:rdbɔ̀:rd] *n.*

Cardboard is a material made out of stiff paper. It is often used to make boxes.
→ *We packed our things into **cardboard** boxes and moved to our new home.*

dilemma [dilémə] *n.*

A **dilemma** is a difficult situation in which a choice has to be made.
→ *Choosing either the tastier or healthier drink proved to be quite a **dilemma**.*

elaborate [ilæbərit] *adj.*

When something is **elaborate**, it contains a lot of details.
→ *She gave the teacher an **elaborate** explanation of her project.*

facilitate [fəsilətèit] *v.*

To **facilitate** something is to make it easier.
→ *To **facilitate** the meeting, Melissa used a simple computer program.*

fleet [fli:t] *n.*

A **fleet** is a group of ships.
→ *The **fleet** of ships spent a few days at the dock.*

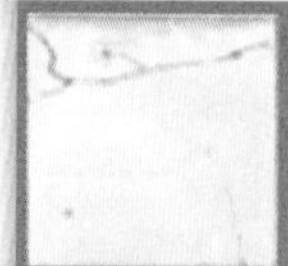

grid [grid] *n.*

A **grid** is a pattern of squares with numbers and letters to find places on a map.
→ *We located our town using the **grid**.*

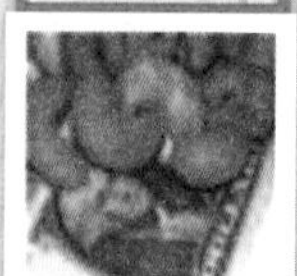

import [impɔ̀:rt] *v.*

To **import** means to bring in a product from another country.
→ *Foods that have been **imported** are usually more expensive.*

infer [infə́:r] *v.*

To **infer** something is to decide it is true based on other information one has.
→ *By the position of the sun in the sky, she **inferred** that it was noon.*

inflate [infléit] *v.*

To **inflate** something means to fill it up with air.
→ *I helped him **inflate** the balloons.*

innate [inéit] *adj.*

When something is **innate**, it is something that one is born with, it is not learned.
→ *He had the **innate** desire to please his teachers.*

marble [mɑ́:rbəl] *n.*

Marble is a type of rock that feels cold and is smooth when cut.
→ *The large house had floors made of **marble**.*

mast [mæst] *n.*

A **mast** is a long pole on a ship that holds the sail.
→ *The **mast** held both sails of the ship upright.*

nausea [nɔ́:ziə] *n.*

Nausea is the feeling of being sick to your stomach.
→ *The doctor said the medicine would help get rid of her **nausea**.*

naval [néivəl] *adj.*

When something is **naval**, it relates to a country's navy or military ships.
→ *The country sent all of its **naval** forces to protect them.*

pouch [pautʃ] *n.*

A **pouch** is a small, flexible bag that is usually made of cloth.
→ *I keep my money in a small **pouch**.*

saturated [sætʃəreitid] *adj.*

If something is **saturated**, it is completely wet.
→ *Leigh's hair became **saturated** in the rain storm.*

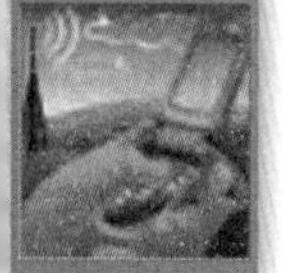

update [ʌpdéit] *n.*

An **update** is an act of making something more modern.
→ *I'm doing an **update** on my personal phone directory.*

Exercise 1

Choose the answer that best fits the question.

1. What is marble often used to for?
   a. To make cars
   b. To make boats
   c. To make statues
   d. To make fires

2. Accessories like earrings, purses, and _______ often make clothes look nicer.
   a. computers
   b. shoes
   c. eye color
   d. muscles

3. What does it mean to update something?
   a. To put away
   b. To leave as it is
   c. To make more modern
   d. To break

4. What is something that should not be imported?
   a. Fruits
   b. Shoes
   c. Ideas
   d. Diseases

5. Naval forces are designed to _______ a country from danger.
   a. protect
   b. fly
   c. incorporate
   d. lead

Exercise 2

Fill in the blanks with the correct words from the word bank.

Word Bank

adequate	fleet	inflated	inferred	mast
innate	pouch	saturated	facilitate	update

The equipment in the school was so old that Isla 1_____________ that it would not be 2_____________ for students to use.

Marilyn had a(n) 3_____________ love for education.
She read many books to 4_____________ her learning.

Larry took a pen out of the 5_____________ in his backpack and used it to 6_____________ the information on the form.

The 7_____________ was used to being out at sea.
As a result, they didn't mind having their clothes 8_____________ with sea water.

After the fire, nothing was left of the ship except for its tall 9_____________.
Soon, the sailors 10_____________ a rescue boat and sailed to safety.

Exercise 3

Choose the one that is similar in meaning to the given word.

1. adequate
a. smart b. enough c. new d. safe

2. facilitate
a. to make easier b. to do first c. to try once d. to find out

3. elaborate
a. beautiful b. small c. detailed d. welcoming

4. dilemma
a. two parts b. contradiction c. problem d. rescue

5. inflate
a. to fill with air b. to enter c. to put away d. to utilize

6. innate
a. strong b. natural c. evil d. full

7. saturated
a. wet b. likely c. uncommon d. unable to change

8. pouch
a. a costume b. an animal c. a bag d. a part

9. nausea
a. improvement b. strength c. lost d. sickness

10. fleet
a. shipbuilder b. structure c. group d. underwater

Exercise 4

Write C if the italicized word is used correctly. Write I if the word is used incorrectly.

1. ____ The *cardboard* box was made from a tough metal.

2. ____ The man had an *acquisition* for being mean to the people that he met.

3. ____ The man helped the old woman *infer* the large object on the shelf.

4. ____ We used the *grid* on the map to help us locate the museum.

5. ____ The painting was *elaborate*. The artist paid attention to every detail.

The Big Ship

Ernest looked at his **fleet** of ships. Usually, he used them for his firm, which **imported marble** statues from other countries. But today he was going fishing. And the ship he chose was his favorite. It had an **elaborate** painting on the side that showed a **naval** battle. It also had some new **updates** to its computer system. His favorite ship's latest **acquisition** was a device with a small **grid** to show the ship's exact location. This new **accessory** kept Ernest from getting lost.

At daybreak, Ernest happily sailed the temperate waters until he was far from land. Then he saw a small boat in the distance. There was an old man standing next to its **mast**. He was waving his arms in the air. There was also a boy with his head hanging over the boat's edge. Ernest **inferred** that the boy was suffering from **nausea**. Both of their clothes were **saturated** with sea water. Ernest assumed that they were in trouble. Most people never realized, but Ernest had an **innate** desire to help people. He began sailing toward them, eager to **facilitate** their rescue and thus solve their **dilemma**.

As he got closer to the boat, he was shocked by its simplicity. The boat's wood looked no stronger than **cardboard**, and the equipment was old. Still, there were several large fish in a **pouch** in the boat.

Ernest threw a large package onto the boat. He yelled, "Here! You can **inflate** this boat to get you back to land."

"Get out of here!" screamed the old man.

Ernest was confused. "Don't you need help?" he asked. "Your ship doesn't seem **adequate** enough to sail so far away from land."

"You've just scared away a huge fish," the boy said. "We waved to let you know you were too close to us."

Ernest turned around and headed home. He learned that it's better not to help unless asked to. Otherwise, you might not help anyone at all.

Reading Comprehension

PART A Mark each statement T for true or F for false. Rewrite the false statements to make them true.

1. ____ Ernest usually used his fleet for his firm that imported marble statues from other countries.

____

2. ____ His favorite ship had updated accessories like a new grid.

____

3. ____ When Ernest saw the old man standing next to the mast, he decided to go home.

____

4. ____ Ernest offered the man and the boy a boat that inflates to facilitate their rescue.

____

5. ____ Ernest had the innate desire to make a lot of money.

____

PART B Answer the questions.

1. What was on the side of Ernest's favorite ship?

____

____

2. How does the author describe the clothes of the people in the boat?

____

____

3. What did Ernest think was wrong with the boy?

____

____

4. Where did the people in the small boat keep their fish?

____

____

5. What did Ernest learn at the end of the story?

____

____

UNIT 16

Word List

addict [ǽdikt] *n.*

An **addict** is a person who cannot stop doing or having something.
→ *She was a coffee* ***addict****. She had more than three cups each day.*

archeological [ɑ̀:rkiəlɑ́dʒikəl] *adj.*

When something is **archeological**, it relates to archeology.
→ *They found* ***archeological*** *evidence that proved an ancient species of man.*

archeology [ɑ̀:rkiɑ́lədʒi] *n.*

Archeology is the study of ancient people through their artifacts.
→ *He studied* ***archeology*** *to learn more about ancient Egyptian culture.*

brainstorm [bréinstɔ̀:rm] *v.*

To **brainstorm** is to have a lot of ideas about a certain topic.
→ *The students met after school to* ***brainstorm*** *ideas for their assignment.*

budget [bʌ́dʒit] *n.*

A **budget** is the amount of money available to spend on something.
→ *His* ***budget*** *for food was very tight.*

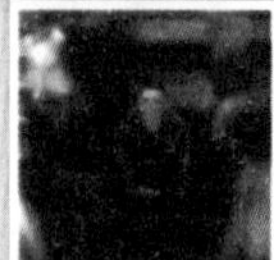

chaotic [keiɑ́tik] *adj.*

When something is **chaotic**, it is crazy, confused, and hectic.
→ *The first day of school can be* ***chaotic*** *for a new student.*

cite [sait] *v.*

To **cite** something is to mention it as an example or as proof of something.
→ *She* ***cited*** *six reasons that the school needed to build new classrooms.*

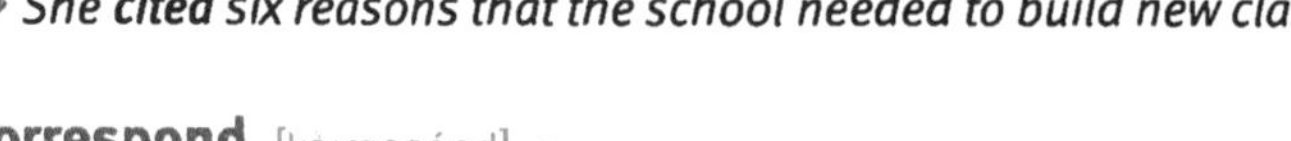

correspond [kɔ̀:rəspɑ́nd] *v.*

To **correspond** is to match or to be similar to something.
→ *The boy's story didn't* ***correspond*** *with his mother's version.*

courtyard [kɔ́:rtjɑ̀:rd] *n.*

A **courtyard** is an outdoor area that is surrounded by the walls of a building.
→ *During the summer, the* ***courtyard*** *is a nice place to have lunch.*

estate [istéit] *n.*

An **estate** is a large area of land owned by a family or organization.
→ *He lived on his father's* ***estate*** *in the country.*

fraud [frɔːd] *n.*

Fraud is the crime of gaining money by lying or by tricking people.

→ *Experts say that credit card **fraud** increases around the holidays.*

hydrogen [háidrədʒən] *n.*

Hydrogen is a gas that has no taste, color, or smell.

→ *Balloons filled with **hydrogen** can easily float away if you aren't careful.*

integrity [intégrəti] *n.*

Integrity is honesty and good morals.

→ *The principal had a lot of **integrity**.*

knit [nit] *v.*

To **knit** is to make fabric by connecting strings together.

→ *My grandmother **knitted** me a sweater.*

outlook [áutlùk] *n.*

An **outlook** is a person's opinion or way of thinking about something.

→ *He changed his **outlook** about rats after he read a book about them.*

parachute [pǽrəʃùːt] *n.*

A **parachute** is a device that helps people and things fall to the ground safely.

→ *They used **parachutes** dropped from airplanes to send supplies to the civilians.*

prehistoric [priːhistɔ́ːrik] *adj.*

When something is **prehistoric**, it is from a time when there was no written history.

→ *The scientists found **prehistoric** pots used by the people in the area.*

proponent [prəpóunənt] *n.*

A **proponent** is a person who supports an idea or a plan.

→ *He was a **proponent** of using environmentally friendly products.*

refine [rifáin] *v.*

To **refine** something is to make it better by making changes.

→ *The principal **refined** his method of controlling students over the years.*

restrict [ristríkt] *v.*

To **restrict** is to limit something and prevent it from getting bigger.

→ *The club **restricted** the amount of members.*

Exercise 1

Choose the answer that best fits the question.

1. Someone with integrity ________.
   a. invents new things
   b. tricks people
   c. lies
   d. is honest

2. What does a person with a good understanding of a budget take care of?
   a. Their safety
   b. Their possessions
   c. Their money
   d. Their pet

3. Which of the following might an archeological expert be interested in?
   a. Reading about ancient devices
   b. Studying the effects of height and speed
   c. Learning how to save lives
   d. Finding his car keys

4. What does it mean to be a parachute addict?
   a. To want to be on land
   b. To want to jump from a plane with a parachute
   c. To always ride in hot-air balloons
   d. To want to be at sea

5. In order to refine an invention, one has to ________.
   a. spend money on it
   b. make it better
   c. be ignorant
   d. know Italian

Exercise 2

Write a word that is similar in meaning to the underlined part.

1. The teacher held classes in the <u>outdoor area surrounded by walls</u> on warm days.

   ____

2. The airport is usually <u>hectic</u> on Saturdays because many people were traveling.

   ____

3. The teacher made sure the correct answers <u>matched</u> with the questions on the test.

   ____

4. The student <u>gave an example from</u> an interview she heard on the radio.

   ____

5. The victim of the <u>crime of tricking</u> told the police about her experience.

   ____

Exercise 3

Choose the one that is similar in meaning to the given word.

1. prehistoric
a. large b. old c. upsetting d. under

2. outlook
a. outside b. plan c. work d. viewpoint

3. proponent
a. supporter b. teacher c. traveler d. scientist

4. estate
a. gas b. property c. airplane d. evidence

5. brainstorm
a. to come up with b. to read a lot c. to get wet d. to jump

Exercise 4

Write C if the italicized word is used correctly. Write I if the word is used incorrectly.

1. _____ The farmer lived on a large *estate*. It was given to him by his father.

2. _____ The principal was a *proponent* of group learning. He wanted students to learn on their own.

3. _____ He wanted to *refine* the machine before he sold it. He spent three years improving it.

4. _____ The seat belt *restricted* the child's movement in the car. He was able to move a lot.

5. _____ After an accident in the laboratory, *hydrogen* filled the air. The gas was completely invisible.

6. _____ The boy had a different *outlook* than his brother. He thought that people should try to save the environment, but his brother thought it wasn't worth trying.

7. _____ The scientists found many *archeological* items in the desert. It would help them study modern societies.

8. _____ Brian *brainstormed* with his group. After an hour, they came up with a great idea.

9. _____ The people in the plane crash were saved by *parachutes*. They dropped safely to the ground using the device.

10. _____ Ellen wanted to learn how to *knit*. She wanted to save people from fires.

11. _____ The man was found guilty of *fraud*. He told people he was selling medicine, but it was only river water.

12. _____ The woman showed her *integrity* by lying to the police about her involvement in the crime.

13. _____ The chocolate *addict* ate chocolate bars about once a month.

14. _____ The *archeology* expert was called to study some ancient bones. They are thought to belong to dinosaurs.

15. _____ The children ran into the *courtyard* when it started raining. They didn't want to get wet.

The History of Parachutes

Scientists who study **archeology** say that there may be some evidence of **prehistoric parachutes**. But the first written history of the device comes from China about 2,100 years ago. Scientists **cite** an ancient book that describes parachutes. However, there is no **archeological** evidence that proves that an actual parachute was ever made. Later, people from northern Africa and Italy also had ideas about a similar invention. In fact, a Leonardo Da Vinci's drawing **corresponds** closely with the modern parachute design!

In 1783, French scientist Sebastian Lenormand invented the first modern parachute. Sebastian **brainstormed** with other scientists to come up with a way to help people jump safely out of burning buildings. He thought the solution was to give people an object to **restrict** their speed while they traveled toward the ground. Many people thought that he was up to some kind of **fraud**, but Sebastian had a lot of **integrity**. His **budget** was limited, so he first tested his theory by using two umbrellas. He jumped out of a tree and found that the umbrellas worked. Next, he **refined** his invention. Rather than using umbrellas, he **knit** a large parachute. Finally, he jumped off a tall building on a French **estate** and landed safely in the **courtyard**.

Sebastian's work gave another man an idea. Jean-Pierre Blanchard had a different **outlook** than Sebastian. He was a hot air balloon **addict**. He was one of the first people to ride in a hot air balloon powered by **hydrogen** gas. He was a **proponent** of using the parachutes to exit from hot air balloons. Starting in 1785, he used his dog to show that animals could land safely from hot air balloons by using parachutes. Then, in 1793, he was faced with a **chaotic** experience. The hot air balloon he was riding in burst and started to fall. He was forced to use a parachute himself. And much to his relief, it saved his life!

Reading Comprehension

PART A Mark each statement T for true or F for false. Rewrite the false statements to make them true.

1. ____ Archeological evidence shows there were prehistoric parachutes in China.

   ____

2. ____ Archeology experts cite an old Chinese book that describes a parachute that corresponds with modern parachutes.

   ____

3. ____ Sebastian brainstormed with scientists to invent a device that would allow people to jump from buildings safely.

   ____

4. ____ On Sebastian's first jump, he used a large blanket to restrict his speed as he traveled to the ground.

   ____

5. ____ Jean-Pierre was a hot air balloon addict.

   ____

PART B Answer the questions.

1. Why did Sebastian use umbrellas on his first jump?

   ____

   ____

2. What did Sebastian think that a parachute would do?

   ____

   ____

3. Where did Sebastian jump with the parachute he refined and knitted?

   ____

   ____

4. How was Jean-Pierre's outlook different from Sebastian?

   ____

   ____

5. Why did Jean-Pierre jump from his hot air balloon?

   ____

   ____

UNIT

17

Word List

attorney [ətə:rni] *n.*

An **attorney** is one who gives others advice about the law.

→ *The **attorney** appeared in front of the judge for me.*

chronic [kránik] *adj.*

When something is **chronic**, it happens over and over again over time.

→ *He had **chronic** pain in his chest and needed to see a doctor.*

discipline [disəplin] *n.*

Discipline is training that helps people follow the rules.

→ *One of the teacher's jobs is to teach her students **discipline**.*

donor [dounər] *n.*

A **donor** is somebody who gives something to an organization.

→ *He was proud to be a blood **donor**.*

fellow [félou] *n.*

A **fellow** is someone who shares a job or quality with someone else.

→ *All of my **fellow** patients at the hospital have also complained about the food.*

gossip [gásip] *n.*

Gossip is information that might be untrue but is still discussed anyway.

→ *The friends exchanged **gossip** about the people they knew in school.*

graduate [grædʒuèit] *v.*

To **graduate** from a school means to complete and pass all courses of study ther

→ *At the end of the spring, my friends and I will **graduate** from high school.*

graffiti [grəfí:ti:] *n.*

Graffiti is words or drawings in public places.

→ *The wall was covered with colorful **graffiti**.*

guardian [gá:rdiən] *n.*

A **guardian** is someone who protects somebody or something.

→ *The librarians are the **guardians** of the books.*

implicate [impləkeit] *v.*

To **implicate** someone is to show that they have done a crime or something ba

→ *The man was **implicated** in the theft at the store.*

kin [kin] *n.*

Kin is a person's family and relatives.

→ *His **kin** were all farmers.*

referee [rèfəri:] *n.*

A **referee** is a person who makes sure that the rules are followed in sports.

→ *The soccer player didn't agree with the **referee**.*

sever [sevə:r] *v.*

To **sever** something is to cut through it completely.

→ *He **severed** the string using scissors.*

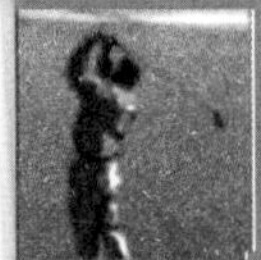

shaft [ʃæft] *n.*

A **shaft** is a handle of a tool or weapon.

→ *The golf club had a long wooden **shaft** that he held in his hands.*

stab [stæb] *v.*

To **stab** means to cut someone or something with a sharp object like a knife.

→ *He **stabbed** the fork into the potato and passed it to his daughter.*

stimulus [stímjələs] *n.*

A **stimulus** is something that causes growth or activity.

→ *Having a lot of money is a **stimulus** for people to buy more things.*

suspicion [səspíʃən] *n.*

A **suspicion** is a feeling that something is possible or true in a crime.

→ *The police had a **suspicion** that the driver had stolen the purse.*

terminate [tə́:rmənèit] *v.*

To **terminate** something means to stop or end it.

→ *The trip was **terminated** after the car broke down.*

theme [θi:m] *n.*

A **theme** is the main subject of a book, movie, or painting.

→ *The students discussed the book's **theme** in class.*

tuition [tju:íʃən] *n.*

Tuition is the amount of money paid to go to a school.

→ *University **tuitions** have increased by fifty percent in the last five years.*

Exercise 1

Choose the answer that best fits the question.

1. Which is a place that you would graduate from?
   a. An island
   b. A school
   c. A house
   d. A party
2. Which of the following has a shaft?
   a. A calendar
   b. A keyboard
   c. A basketball
   d. A pool stick
3. What is one responsibility of a referee?
   a. To make sure a game is fair
   b. To stop crime
   c. To guard athletes
   d. To be a good parent
4. Why might somebody hire an attorney?
   a. To watch security tapes
   b. To pay for their bills
   c. To prove they didn't do a crime
   d. To help them decorate their home
5. How would you describe chronic pain?
   a. It hurts a lot.
   b. It hurts all the time.
   c. It hurts in the morning.
   d. It hurts only when it is cold.

Exercise 2

Choose the one that is similar in meaning to the given word.

1. kin
   a. relatives b. boxes c. friends d. principals
2. chronic
   a. useless b. unskilled c. constant d. again
3. attorney
   a. police officer b. lawyer c. teacher d. instructor
4. gossip
   a. plans b. an untrue talk c. culture d. evil
5. sever
   a. to watch b. to cut off c. to keep d. to hit
6. stab
   a. to cut b. to prove c. to get help d. to wonder
7. theme
   a. a book b. a preview c. a main idea d. a perspective
8. suspicion
   a. lunch money b. classes c. mistrust d. clothes
9. guardian
   a. a protector b. a judge c. intelligence d. truth
10. terminate
    a. to wait b. to end c. to destroy d. to hurt

Exercise 3

Fill in the blanks with the correct words from the word bank.

tuition	chronic	graffiti	discipline	gossip
terminate	stimulus	donor	graduated	implicated

Mr. Wilson 1______________ from the university over 15 years ago.
He has always been a generous 2______________ and wants to improve the school.

The university recently decreased its 3______________.
It was supposed to be a 4______________ for more students to study there.

Laurie was 5______________ in a terrible thing.
She was caught leaving 6______________ on the school wall.

Elliot had 7______________ problems at school.
His parents decided to show more 8______________.

Hannah was tired of hearing 9______________ about her neighbors.
She decided to 10______________ that behavior and think about better things.

Exercise 4

Write C if the italicized word is used correctly. Write I if the word is used incorrectly.

1. ____ I may not be able to go to college next year. I don't have enough money for *tuition*.
2. ____ The boy's parents didn't know how to control him. They taught him *discipline*.
3. ____ He was a *donor*. He received gifts from people all of the time.
4. ____ His new stove will be a *stimulus* for him to cook at home more often.
5. ____ Ellen didn't like the color of her walls, so she painted *graffiti* on them.
6. ____ Jason was *implicated* in the bank robbery. Several people saw him do it.
7. ____ Besides her parents, Olivia had no other *kin*. She only had one sister.
8. ____ The gardener picked up the tool by the *shaft*. It was easiest to hold that way.
9. ____ The man was sent to prison for *stabbing* someone. The person was hurt but survived.
10. ____ The *theme* of the book was forgiveness.
11. ____ Leslie's father is a policeman. He is a *guardian* of crime.
12. ____ I took a knife and *severed* the line from the pole to the fish's mouth.
13. ____ The food was being held on *suspicion* of committing two crimes in the city.
14. ____ I spoke to my *fellow* teachers, and we all agreed to support the students at the rally.
15. ____ The *referee* said the player had broken the rules.

"I Didn't Do It!"

Billy was in big trouble. The day before, a **donor** gave the school a painting with a sports **theme**. It showed a **referee** congratulating two athletes. The principal hung the painting in front of the office, hoping that it would be a **stimulus** for students to play sports. The next morning, however, the painting was destroyed. There was **graffiti** on it, and it had many holes in it. The worst part was that one of Billy's **fellow** students said she thought she saw Billy do it!

But Billy didn't do it. The principal called Billy's parents and said, "Billy won't tell us the truth. He's a **chronic** liar, and he ruined the painting. If you don't pay for it, we'll **terminate** his education here."

Billy's parents didn't have enough money to pay for the painting and for his **tuition**. But Billy's parents had an idea. That afternoon, they went to see Mr. Meyers, an **attorney**.

"Mr. Meyers, my son has been **implicated** in a crime he says he didn't do," Billy's father said. "Everybody believes the **gossip**. Even some of our own **kin** think he did it!"

"I believe you. My **suspicion** is that the tape from the security cameras will show who really did it," said Mr. Meyers.

The next day, Mr. Meyers received a packet with the videotape from the school. It showed another student who resembled Billy walking up to the painting and writing on it. Then the student took a knife by the **shaft** and started to **stab** large holes in it. Finally, he **severed** the rope that held up the painting, and it fell to the floor.

Mr. Meyers showed the tape to the principal. "Clearly, that's not Billy," he said. "This boy is actually responsible and needs some **discipline**."

Billy was happy that someone believed him. He said to Mr. Meyers, "When I **graduate** and go to university, I will major in law, so I can be a **guardian** of justice like you!"

Reading Comprehension

PART A Mark each statement T for true or F for false. Rewrite the false statements to make them true.

1. ____ A donor gave the school a painting with a sports theme as a stimulus for students to play sports.

   ____

2. ____ The painting showed a referee congratulating two athletes.

   ____

3. ____ Billy was implicated in the crime because a fellow student received a packet with a videotape showing him doing it.

   ____

4. ____ Everybody gossiped about Billy, and even some of our kin think he did it.

   ____

5. ____ The principal threatened to terminate Billy's education if his parents didn't pay his tuition.

   ____

PART B Answer the questions.

1. What did the principal say about Billy?

   ____

   ____

2. What was Mr. Meyers' suspicion?

   ____

   ____

3. What did the videotape show?

   ____

   ____

4. What did the attorney suggest to the principal about the boy responsible for the crime?

   ____

   ____

5. Why did Billy say he wanted his major to be law when he went to university?

   ____

   ____

UNIT 18

Word List

aggressive [əgrésiv] *adj.*

If someone is **aggressive,** then they constantly want to fight.

→ *Nobody liked to play games with him because he was always too **aggressive**.*

amnesty [æmnəsti] *n.*

Amnesty is a pardon given to prisoners of war.

→ *She was denied **amnesty** for her involvement in the war.*

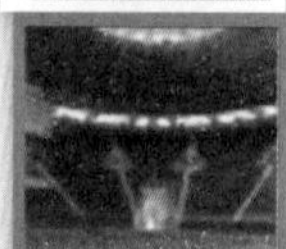

arena [əri:nə] *n.*

An **arena** is a building where people can watch sports and concerts.

→ *The new **arena** was all set to hold the championship match.*

auditorium [ɔ̀:ditɔ́:riəm] *n.*

An **auditorium** is a large building used for public events.

→ *People have gathered at the school **auditorium** to watch the play.*

captive [kǽptiv] *n.*

A **captive** is a prisoner.

→ *The guards told the **captive** that there was no way he could escape the prison.*

combat [kámbæt] *n.*

Combat is fighting between two people or groups.

→ *The two warriors were locked in **combat**.*

commonplace [kámənplèis] *adj.*

If something is **commonplace,** then it is ordinary.

→ *There is nothing **commonplace** about the way Morris dresses.*

compound [kámpaund] *n.*

A **compound** is an enclosed area such as a prison or factory.

→ *The workers waited outside the **compound** for the gates to the factory to open.*

corps [kɔ:r] *n.*

A **corps** is a division of a military force.

→ *The army had a **corps** of archers who trained apart from the regular soldiers.*

distract [distrǽkt] *v.*

To **distract** someone means to stop them from concentrating on something.

→ *The phone call **distracted** him so much that he forgot all about his homework.*

dumb [dʌm] *adj.*

If someone is **dumb**, they are unable to speak.

→ *She did not share the secret. She remained silent as if she were* ***dumb.***

foe [fou] *n.*

A **foe** is an enemy or opponent.

→ *It was hard to believe that anyone could be his* ***foe.***

hack [hæk] *v.*

To **hack** something means to cut it into uneven pieces.

→ *My uncle used the ax to* ***hack*** *the tree into many logs.*

meditate [médətèit] *v.*

To **meditate** means to focus or think deeply in silence.

→ *She liked to* ***meditate*** *for several hours of each day.*

nick [nik] *v.*

To **nick** someone means to cut them slightly with a sharp object.

→ *While cutting the carrots, the cook* ***nicked*** *his finger with the edge of his knife.*

provoke [prəvóuk] *v.*

To **provoke** someone means to annoy them on purpose to cause violence.

→ *The older boy* ***provoked*** *Paul by calling him mean names.*

realm [relm] *n.*

A **realm** is any area of activity or interest.

→ *He was not very active in the* ***realm*** *of business.*

reign [rein] *n.*

A **reign** is the period of time in which a ruler rules.

→ *The emperor's* ***reign*** *lasted for only two years.*

rust [rʌst] *n.*

Rust is a red and brown coating on iron objects caused by water and air.

→ *The old metal gate would not swing because the hinges were covered in* ***rust.***

sacred [séikrid] *adj.*

If something is **sacred**, then it is worshipped and respected.

→ *One religion in India will not harm cows because it believes that they are* ***sacred.***

Exercise 1

Choose the answer that best fits the question.

1. Who would most likely serve in a corps?
   a. A teacher b. A baby c. A minister d. A soldier
2. What would you find near a compound?
   a. A fence b. A napkin
   c. A parade d. A computer program
3. Which would you most likely see in an auditorium?
   a. A shark b. A river c. A crowd d. Birds
4. Who would most likely be involved in combat?
   a. A warrior b. A teacher c. A swimmer d. A dancer
5. Which of the following is a dumb thing to do?
   a. To go swimming b. To chop wood
   c. To play with matches d. To trim your fingernails

Exercise 2

Choose the one that is opposite in meaning to the given word.

1. foe
   a. shovel b. friend c. room d. thumb
2. amnesty
   a. education b. prison c. energy d. highway
3. combat
   a. peace b. brush c. carpet d. bird
4. sacred
   a. brave b. better c. evil d. warm
5. distract
   a. increase b. pretend c. return d. focus
6. dumb
   a. kind b. wrong c. loud d. hurt
7. commonplace
   a. unusual b. fresh c. pleasant d. actual
8. hack
   a. mend b. sneeze c. blame d. dig
9. aggressive
   a. smart b. tall c. calm d. young
10. provoke
   a. mash b. burn c. tire d. soothe

Exercise 3

Choose the one that is similar in meaning to the given word.

1. realm
   a. lunch b. area c. gown d. idea
2. auditorium
   a. market b. assembly hall c. music d. present
3. rust
   a. morning b. speed c. truth d. decay
4. corps
   a. basin b. troop c. pace d. image
5. meditate
   a. think b. bake c. swim d. sweep
6. compound
   a. garbage b. pasture c. kilogram d. camp
7. reign
   a. bath b. snow c. rule d. chalk
8. arena
   a. stadium b. boulder c. camera d. believable
9. nick
   a. scratch b. choice c. grain d. glove
10. captive
   a. challenge b. motor c. prisoner d. ticket

Exercise 4

Write C if the italicized word is used correctly. Write I if the word is used incorrectly.

1. ____ The *arena* was filled with adoring fans.
2. ____ The wooden fence was covered in a thick layer of *rust*.
3. ____ His *reign* only lasted three years before he became sick and passed away.
4. ____ You will like Jack. You both have so much *commonplace* together.
5. ____ Her perfume was too strong. I was *distracted* by it during the meeting.

The Soldier's Decision

A soldier was captured while fighting in an enemy king's land. It was well known that this king would make **captives** fight one another. This was **commonplace** during his **reign**. For these fights, the king had built several large **arenas**. He often awarded the winners by setting them free or even having them join his elite army **corps**.

The soldier, however, decided he had seen too much violence. He now felt that all life was **sacred**. The night before his first match, he made a risky decision. He decided that he would not engage in **combat**. He knew he may never be set free, but it was a decision that he was willing to accept.

In the morning, he was led from the prisoners' **compound** to one of the king's arenas. A gate coated in **rust** stood between him and the **auditorium**'s floor. He was worried, but he knew what he had to do.

When the gate opened, he calmly walked to the center of the arena and sat. He started to **meditate**. His **foe** Darius, who was skilled in the **realm** of sword fighting and was typically not very **aggressive**, would not fight the quiet soldier until he attacked Darius first.

Darius tried to **provoke** him by **hacking** at the air close to his head with his sword. But the soldier was not **distracted**. He sat quietly, as if he were **dumb**, and looked calmly up at the sky. Even when Darius **nicked** him on the cheek with the edge of his sword, the soldier did not move.

At last he threw down his sword and shield and gave up. "I can't fight someone who refuses to fight me!" Darius shouted to the king.

The king was very impressed with the soldier. Never in any battle had he seen someone so brave. As a result, he gave the peaceful soldier **amnesty**. The soldier's actions proved to the king and everyone in the arena that peace was more powerful than fighting.

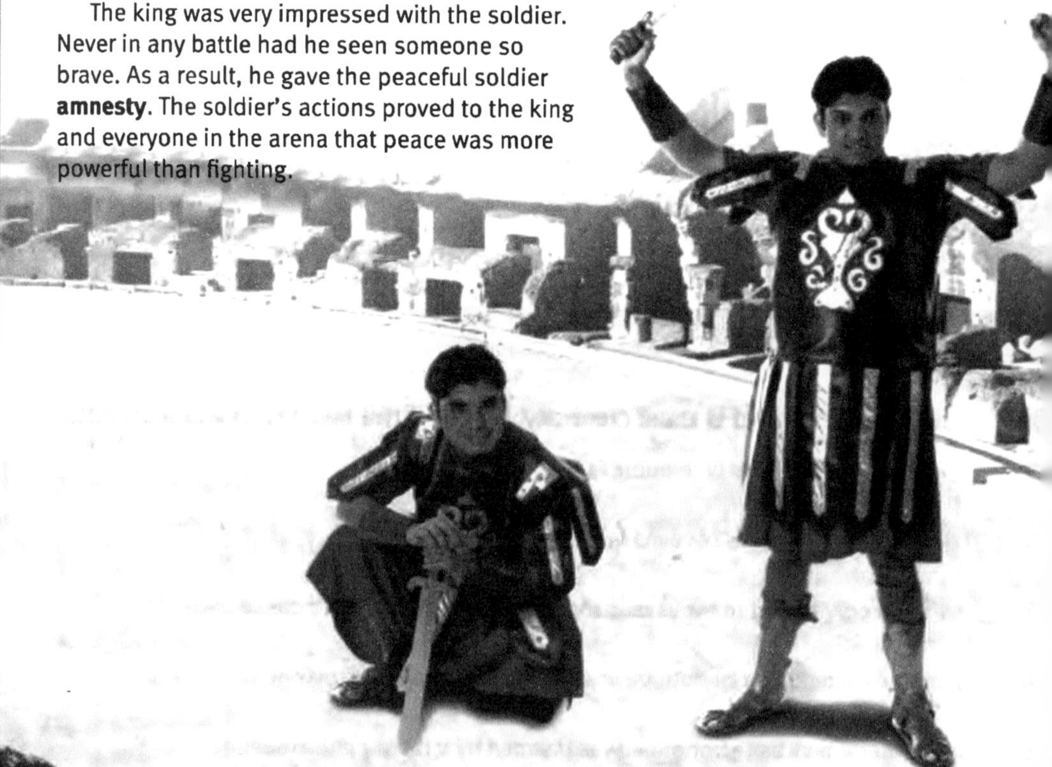

Reading Comprehension

PART A Mark each statement T for true or F for false. Rewrite the false statements to make them true.

1. ____ The gate between the soldier and the auditorium was coated with rust.

____

2. ____ The prisoner was led from the arena to the compound.

____

3. ____ While he meditated, the soldier was distracted by his opponent.

____

4. ____ The king gave the brave soldier amnesty and made him join his elite army corps.

____

5. ____ The quiet soldier felt that all life was sacred.

____

PART B Answer the questions.

1. Why did the captive seem like he was dumb?

____

____

2. What was commonplace during the reign of the enemy king?

____

____

3. In what realm did the soldier's opponent Darius have skill?

____

____

4. Where did the soldier get nicked by his opponent?

____

____

5. What did the quiet soldier prove by refusing to engage his foe in combat?

____

____

UNIT 19

Word List

accordingly [əkɔ́:rdiŋli] *adv.*

If someone acts **accordingly,** they act in a way that is suitable.

→ *He feels like he did a good job, and his boss should pay him* ***accordingly.***

anchor [ǽŋkər] *n.*

An **anchor** is a heavy object dropped from a boat to make it stay in one place.

→ *When the ship reached its destination, the crew dropped the* ***anchor.***

buoy [bú:i] *n.*

A **buoy** is a floating sign that warns boats of dangerous areas.

→ *Don't steer the boat near those* ***buoys.*** *There are rocks underneath the water.*

catastrophe [kətǽstrəfi] *n.*

A **catastrophe** is an unexpected event that causes great suffering or damage.

→ *It was a* ***catastrophe*** *for my family when my dad lost his job.*

context [kántekst] *n.*

Context is the situations that form the background of an event.

→ *They studied the* ***context*** *of the battle before giving their presentation.*

designate [dézignèit] *v.*

To **designate** someone or something means to give them a particular descriptio

→ *The famous lighthouse was* ***designated*** *a historical monument.*

distort [distɔ́:rt] *v.*

To **distort** something means to lie about it.

→ *His lawyer* ***distorted*** *the facts so that he would be set free.*

dock [dɑk] *n.*

A **dock** is an enclosed area where ships go to be loaded, unloaded, and repair

→ *The huge ship pulled into the* ***dock,*** *and the crew unloaded the cargo.*

fore [fɔ:r] *n.*

The **fore** of something is the front part of it.

→ *The teacher's desk is at the* ***fore*** *of the classroom.*

frequent [frí:kwənt] *adj.*

If something is **frequent,** then it happens or is done often.

→ *While Dad was sick, the doctor made* ***frequent*** *visits to his house.*

genuine [dʒénjuin] *adj.*

When something is **genuine**, it is true or real.

→ *After the painting was determined to be **genuine**, it sold for a million dollars.*

grease [griːs] *n.*

Grease is an oily substance put on moving parts, so they work smoothly.

→ *When I was done working on the car, I had **grease** all over my hands.*

intricate [íntrəkit] *adj.*

When something is **intricate**, it has many small parts or details.

→ *The **intricate** painting on the quilt was very lovely.*

offset [ɔ̀ːfsét] *v.*

To **offset** means to use one thing to cancel out the effect of another thing.

→ *Increased wages are **offset** by higher prices for goods.*

overlap [òuvərlǽp] *v.*

To **overlap** something means to cover a piece of it.

→ *The gift on top **overlaps** the other gift on the bottom.*

precipitate [prisípətèit] *v.*

To **precipitate** an event means to cause it to happen sooner than normal.

→ *The violent attack **precipitated** an all-out war.*

secondhand [sékəndhǽnd] *adj.*

When something is **secondhand**, it has been owned by someone else.

→ *Her **secondhand** jeans were a bit faded in the front.*

slot [slɑt] *n.*

A **slot** is a narrow opening in a machine or container.

→ *To operate the machine, put your coins into the **slot**.*

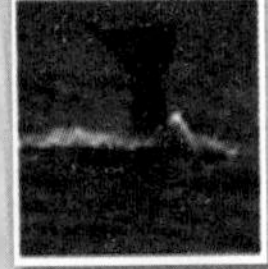

submerge [səbmə́ːrdʒ] *v.*

To **submerge** something means to put it below the surface of a liquid.

→ *The whale **submerged** its huge body into the ocean.*

tactic [tǽktik] *n.*

A **tactic** is a careful plan to achieve something.

→ *Sam thought of a good **tactic** in order to attract more business.*

Exercise 1

Choose the answer that best fits the question.

1. Which person uses an anchor?
   a. A mailman b. A sailor c. A writer d. A priest
2. If your jacket is made of genuine leather, it ________.
   a. is not expensive b. falls apart easily c. is real leather d. it is alive
3. What might precipitate a fight?
   a. Taking a nap b. Sharing lunch c. Doing homework d. Name calling
4. Where would you most likely see a buoy?
   a. On the ocean b. On the street c. At the store d. In an airplane
5. If a problem is frequent, then it happens ________.
   a. several times b. only once c. almost never d. in the afternoon

Exercise 2

Write a word that is similar in meaning to the underlined part.

1. I buy most of my clothes <u>once owned</u>.

   ____

2. The <u>enclosed area in the harbor for loading ships</u> is very busy this time of day.

   ____

3. Be sure not to <u>lie about</u> the facts about the crime. The police need to know everything in order to help us.

   ____

4. The women sat on the <u>front part</u> of the ship and enjoyed the warm sun.

   ____

5. I have to add a stop to our trip, so adjust your plans <u>in a way that depends on the situation</u>.

   ____

6. To understand this show, you have to know the <u>general situation that relates to it</u>.

   ____

7. The new sewing machine was <u>made up of many small parts and details</u>.

   ____

8. Let's hope that our plans do not <u>have a part of one occupying the space of the other</u>.

   ____

9. The city has decided to <u>give a particular description of</u> this area as a non-smoking zone.

   ____

10. I think the gears need a little more <u>oily substance used to make parts work smoothly</u>.

   ____

Exercise 3

Write C if the italicized word is used correctly. Write I if the word is used incorrectly.

1. ____ The key fit perfectly in the *slot*.

2. ____ Jackets help to *offset* the effect of a cold wind.

3. ____ I need to *distort* my homework if I'm going to get it turned in by tomorrow.

4. ____ The parade was a *catastrophe*. It went smoothly, and everyone had a great time.

5. ____ They had to water the tree four times a day. It was a *frequent* chore.

6. ____ The *intricate* bench was just a large, unpainted piece of wood.

7. ____ The weather *precipitates* a great weekend.

8. ____ We walked to the *docks* to watch ships pull in and out.

9. ____ The lion *submerged* out of the bushes and attacked its prey.

10. ____ The *secondhand* book was brand new. I was the first to read it.

11. ____ She was noted for creating some imaginative *tactics* to claim victory.

12. ____ The guide asked us to be very quiet, so we acted *accordingly*.

13. ____ The chef arranged the slices of bread so that they *overlapped* each other.

14. ____ We knew from the beginning that the *genuine* man was not who he claimed to be.

15. ____ The *buoy* over there warns ships that the water is too shallow.

16. ____ We stood at the *fore* of the ship. At the front we could see where we were going.

17. ____ The *grease* made it easy to find a good parking spot.

18. ____ The fireman who saved the family was *designated* the "hero of the month."

19. ____ Check the *context* for spelling errors before you turn it in to the teacher.

20. ____ This looks like a good place to drop the boat's *anchor* and relax in the sun.

Jane's Pride

Jane and her father, Mike, owned a **secondhand** boat. They called it "High Hopes." The two loved to spend time together on the ocean and would often go on long fishing trips.

Mike taught Jane how to perform important tasks. Jane learned how to steer the boat and adjust the sails. She learned how to put **grease** on the **intricate** gears of the motor. She learned how to **submerge** the **anchor** and secure it by putting a rope in a **slot**. Jane liked helping her father, but she thought that she wasn't very good at it. Sometimes, she omitted important steps and made **frequent** mistakes. Jane thought she wasn't capable of manual labor.

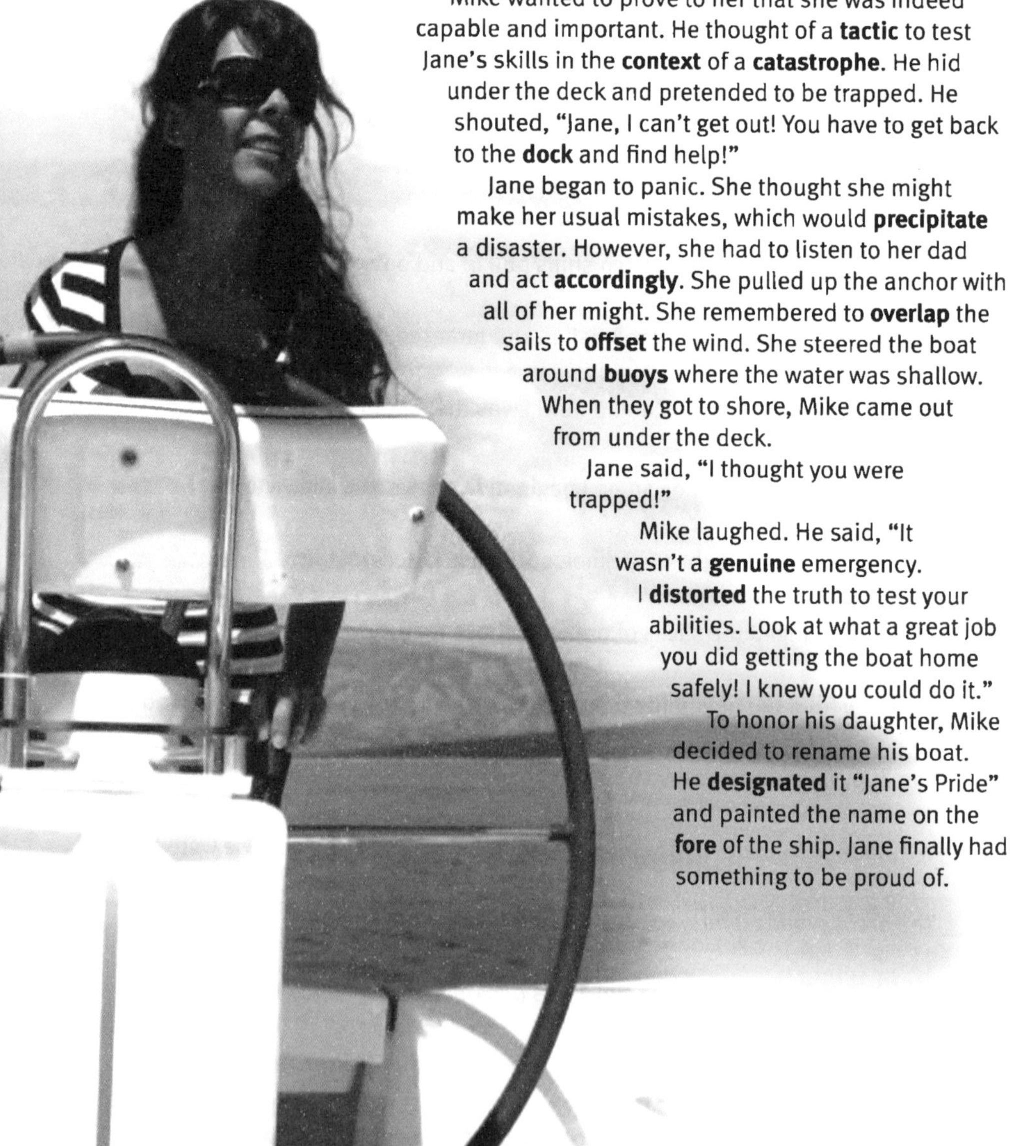

Mike wanted to prove to her that she was indeed capable and important. He thought of a **tactic** to test Jane's skills in the **context** of a **catastrophe**. He hid under the deck and pretended to be trapped. He shouted, "Jane, I can't get out! You have to get back to the **dock** and find help!"

Jane began to panic. She thought she might make her usual mistakes, which would **precipitate** a disaster. However, she had to listen to her dad and act **accordingly**. She pulled up the anchor with all of her might. She remembered to **overlap** the sails to **offset** the wind. She steered the boat around **buoys** where the water was shallow. When they got to shore, Mike came out from under the deck.

Jane said, "I thought you were trapped!"

Mike laughed. He said, "It wasn't a **genuine** emergency. I **distorted** the truth to test your abilities. Look at what a great job you did getting the boat home safely! I knew you could do it."

To honor his daughter, Mike decided to rename his boat. He **designated** it "Jane's Pride" and painted the name on the **fore** of the ship. Jane finally had something to be proud of.

Reading Comprehension

PART A Mark each statement T for true or F for false. Rewrite the false statements to make them true.

1. ____ Jane thought she would precipitate a disaster if she omitted her frequent mistakes.

2. ____ Jane submerged the anchor and secured it by putting a rope in a slot.

3. ____ Jane put grease on the intricate buoy.

4. ____ Mike thought of a tactic to test Jane's skills in the context of a catastrophe.

5. ____ Mike designated the secondhand boat "Jane's Pride."

PART B Answer the questions.

1. Where did Jane have to steer the boat to find help?

2. What was the first thing Jane did after she decided to listen to her dad and act accordingly?

3. On which part of the boat did they paint the name?

4. When Jane overlapped the sails, what was she trying to offset?

5. What was the purpose of Mike deceiving his daughter?

UNIT 20

Word List

aggregate [ǽgrəgit] *adj.*

When a number is **aggregate**, it is made up of smaller amounts added together.

→ *The company totaled its **aggregate** sales for the entire year.*

antibiotic [æ̀ntibaiάtik] *n.*

An **antibiotic** is a medical drug used to kill bacteria and treat infections.

→ *The doctor gave me a shot of an **antibiotic** when I got the flu.*

circuit [sə́:rkit] *n.*

A **circuit** is a piece of an electronic device that allows electricity to flow.

→ *Be very careful not to shock yourself when fixing an electrical **circuit**.*

complement [kάmpləmènt] *v.*

To **complement** something or someone is to make them better.

→ *The wool scarf **complemented** her lovely eyes.*

compress [kəmprès] *v.*

To **compress** something means to press or squeeze it so that it takes up less space.

→ *I **compressed** my clothes to fit into a single suitcase.*

database [déitəbèis] *n.*

A **database** is a collection of data that is stored in a computer.

→ *The company has a **database** of all the names and accounts of their customers.*

equivalent [ikwívələnt] *n.*

An **equivalent** is an amount or value that is the same as another amount or value.

→ *I worked the **equivalent** of sixty hours this week.*

immune [imjú:n] *adj.*

When someone is **immune** to a disease, they cannot be affected by it.

→ *Children usually get shots to make them **immune** to certain diseases.*

input [ínpùt] *n.*

Input is information that is put into a computer.

→ *Type the **input** into the computer program.*

intimate [íntəmit] *adj.*

When a relationship is **intimate**, the two things are very closely connected.

→ *I only tell my secrets to my most **intimate** friends.*

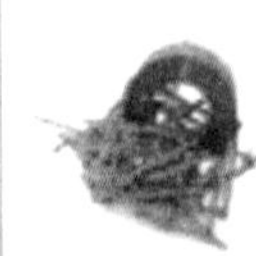

magnet [mæ̀gnit] *n.*

A **magnet** is a piece of iron or other material which attracts iron toward it.

→ *I used a **magnet** to pick up the nails that were scattered on the floor.*

metabolism [mətæ̀bəlizəm] *n.*

A person's **metabolism** is the way chemical processes in their body use energy.

→ *If you exercise every day, your **metabolism** speeds up.*

microchip [máikroutʃìp] *n.*

A **microchip** is a small device inside a computer that holds information.

→ *I can put more data on my computer if I buy a more powerful **microchip**.*

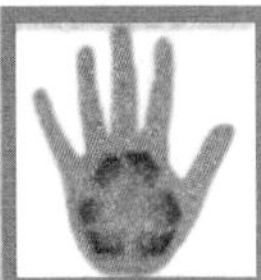

phase [feiz] *n.*

A **phase** is a stage in a process or the gradual development of something.

→ *The first **phase** in the recycling project involves finding volunteers to help out.*

pinch [pintʃ] *v.*

To **pinch** means to take a piece of skin between one's fingers and squeeze.

→ ***I pinched** my nose, so I couldn't smell the odor from the garbage.*

prevalent [prévələnt] *adj.*

When something is **prevalent**, it is common.

→ *Growing a beard is more **prevalent** behavior in men than women.*

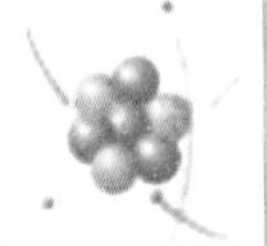

quantum [kwɑ́ntəm] *adj.*

When something is **quantum**, it relates to the behavior of atomic particles.

→ *The physics student studied **quantum** mechanics.*

ratio [réiʃou] *n.*

A **ratio** is a relationship between two things expressed in numbers or amounts.

→ *The boy to girl **ratio** is one to three.*

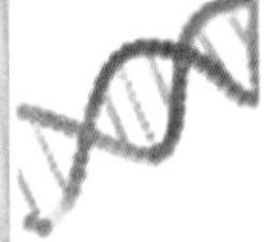

spiral [spáiərəl] *n.*

A **spiral** is a shape which winds round and round in a larger and larger circle.

→ *A strand of DNA looks like two interlocking **spirals**.*

viral [váiərəl] *adj.*

When something is **viral**, it is a disease or infection that is caused by a virus.

→ *The girl was in bed for a week when she had a **viral** infection.*

Exercise 1

Choose the answer that best fits the question.

1. Where would you find a microchip?
a. In a salad
b. In a laptop
c. In a chair
d. In your dog

2. What is found at a quantum level?
a. A comet
b. Atomic particles
c. A scale
d. Biological theories

3. What does a magnet attract?
a. Metal
b. Trees
c. Water
d. Plastic

4. What is an example of a ratio?
a. Rough to smooth
b. Cat to dog
c. Two to one
d. Black and white

5. What is the equivalent of 60 minutes?
a. One hour
b. 30 minutes
c. One day
d. One century

Exercise 2

Fill in the blanks with the correct words from the word bank.

Word Bank				
spiral	database	prevalent	antibiotic	immune
input	ratio	viral	phase	magnet

The doctors just found out that the infection is **1**______________.
Since a virus is not a bacteria, it cannot be treated with a(n) **2**______________.

He looked at the information that was stored in the **3**______________.
After comparing the data, he expressed the results in a **4**______________.

The process of building the house is in the final **5**______________.
The last step is putting in a staircase in the shape of a **6**______________.

We learned what metals are attracted to a **7**______________.
We fed our results into the computer as **8**______________.

In this country, polio is not **9**______________.
It is highly uncommon because most people are **10**______________ thanks to vaccines.

Exercise 3

Write a word that is similar in meaning to the underlined part.

1. Walking was the most common form of transportation in the big city.

   ____

2. We are now ready to begin the first particular stage in the process.

   ____

3. Do the doctors know if the condition is a disease caused by a virus?

   ____

4. Some people don't believe in taking drugs used to treat infections.

   ____

5. We were offered a bottle of sparkling cider to go well with our meal.

   ____

6. I seem to have lost some of the information that is put into a computer.

   ____

7. I wish they wouldn't store personal information in the collection of data in the computer.

   ____

8. His grandmother loves to take a piece of skin and squeeze his cheeks.

   ____

9. I don't really understand my body's way that chemical processes cause food to be used.

   ____

10. A spring looks like a shape which winds round and round.

    ____

Exercise 4

Write C if the italicized word is used correctly. Write I if the word is used incorrectly.

1. ____ The *microchip* was damaged when she spilled water on the computer.
2. ____ *Quantum* mechanics deals with planets and stars.
3. ____ People with fast *metabolisms* are usually thin and in good shape.
4. ____ I *compressed* the sponge into a little ball.
5. ____ You should *pinch* your homework if you want to get it turned in on time.
6. ____ I was amazed by the *aggregate* total of donated gifts and money.
7. ____ The children played all day on the *circuit*.
8. ____ Dressing and pepper *complemented* the tasty salad.
9. ____ *Intimate* friends should not tell lies about each other.
10. ____ This tuba is the *equivalent* of a set of drums.

Microchips

The bond between humans and computers is becoming more **intimate** than ever before. Scientists are now putting **microchips** inside people's bodies. They are made up of **compressed** electrical **circuits** that can detect and record data about the body. They are tiny, but they hold the **equivalent** amount of data as most computers.

A microchip is put to use inside a person with a simple procedure. First, a doctor must put data about the patient onto a chip. **Input** about the person's age, race, gender, and medical history is stored on the chip. The second **phase** of the process involves putting it in the person's skin. The doctor **pinches** a piece of skin and cuts a tiny hole with a tool shaped like a **spiral**. The chip is inserted, and the skin is allowed to heal. At last, it begins the task of putting data into its **database**.

Microchips scan the patient's body to record what is happening on the **quantum** level. They can find problems with the person's **metabolism** and organs. They can also detect **viral** infections. They can find the **aggregate** number of **immune** and infected cells and present the results in a **ratio**. They can even tell doctors what type of **antibiotic** to give to the patient!

To recover the chip's data, the doctor uses a special **magnet** that copies it. This way, the doctor can put the information from the chip onto a computer. Then they can find out exactly what is wrong with the person.

The idea of putting chips in humans is still very new. However, it is now becoming more **prevalent**. Scientists and doctors are hopeful about the future uses of microchips. Someday, all new babies might get a microchip soon after they are born. Doctors will be able to know about any problems from the very beginning. It is obvious that medicine and computers **complement** each other well.

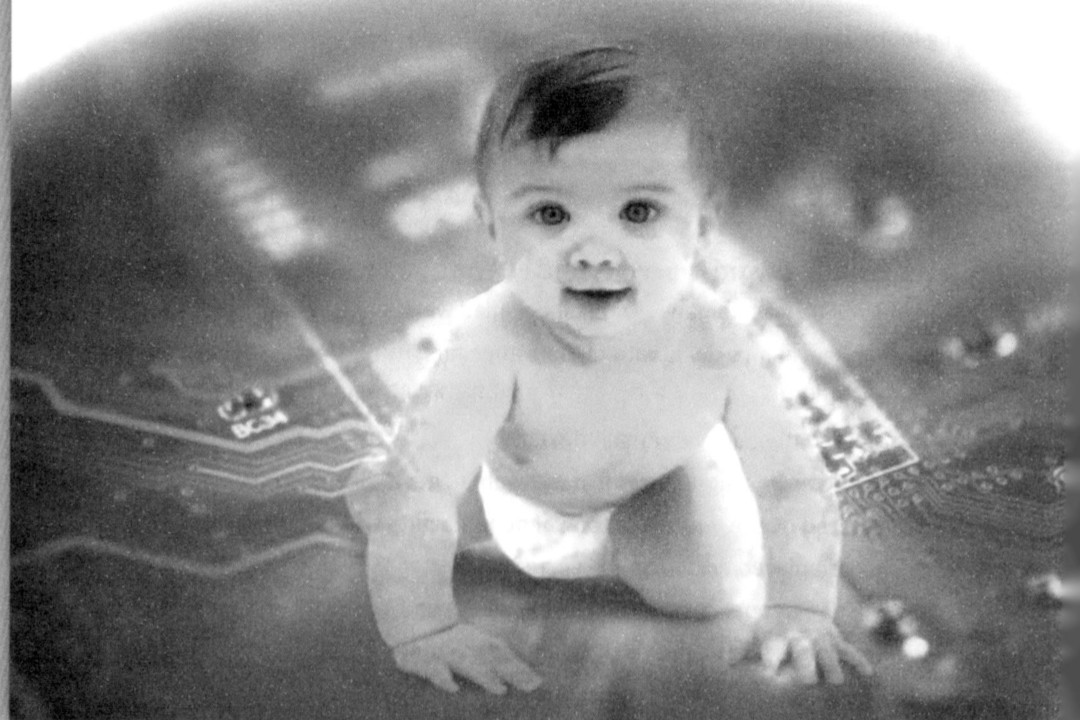

Reading Comprehension

PART A **Mark each statement T for true or F for false. Rewrite the false statements to make them true.**

1. ____ Microchips are made up of compressed electrical circuits.

   ____

2. ____ Chips express the aggregate number of immune and intimate cells in a ratio.

   ____

3. ____ Chips detect viral infections and problems with people's metabolism.

   ____

4. ____ A doctor pinches the skin and cuts a hole with a tool shaped like a spiral.

   ____

5. ____ Putting antibiotics in humans is becoming more prevalent.

   ____

PART B **Answer the questions.**

1. What does the doctor's special magnet do?

   ____

   ____

2. What holds the equivalent amount of storage as most computers?

   ____

   ____

3. After the input is stored on the chip, what is the next phase of the process?

   ____

   ____

4. What do microchips do to record what is happening on the quantum level?

   ____

   ____

5. What complements each other, according to the passage?

   ____

   ____

UNIT 21

Word List

astounded [əstáundid] *adj.*

If you are **astounded**, you are very surprised.

→ *I was **astounded** that Monica won the art competition.*

attribute [ǽtribjù:t] *n.*

An **attribute** is a characteristic of a person or thing.

→ *He isn't very clever, but he does have some other positive **attributes**.*

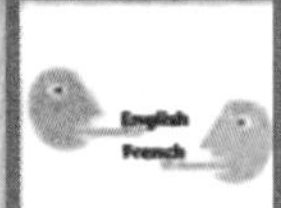

bilingual [bailíŋgwəl] *adj.*

If someone is **bilingual**, then they can speak two languages.

→ *Since you already know English, after learning French you'll be **bilingual**.*

clone [kloun] *n.*

A **clone** is an identical copy of a living creature.

→ *Scientists recently made a **clone** of a sheep.*

colloquial [kəlóukwiəl] *adj.*

Colloquial describes informal words that are more suitable for speech than writing.

→ *I find it difficult to understand people if they use **colloquial** language.*

cosmetics [kɑzmétiks] *n.*

Cosmetics are substances that make the face and skin more beautiful.

→ *Girls often look nicer when they don't use so many **cosmetics**.*

dash [dæʃ] *v.*

To **dash** means to run or move quickly.

→ *Helen **dashed** up the stairs, so she wouldn't be late for her appointment.*

disgust [disgʌ́st] *n.*

Disgust is a feeling of distaste and anger caused by something rude or unpleasant.

→ *He felt **disgust** toward his date because she had such terrible eating habits.*

fluorescent [flùərésnt] *adj.*

If something is **fluorescent**, it is such a bright color that it seems to give off light.

→ *She highlighted the key words in the document with a **fluorescent** yellow pen.*

furious [fjúəriəs] *adj.*

If you are **furious**, you are extremely angry.

→ *My father was **furious** when he read my bad school report.*

gulf [gʌlf] *n.*

A **gulf** is a gap between people who do not understand each other.

→ *There has been a **gulf** between James and Tony since their parents died.*

humanities [hju:mænətiz] *n.*

Humanities are subjects which analyze human ideas, such as history and literature.

→ *Jennifer has always been more interested in **humanities** than science.*

knot [nɑt] *n.*

A **knot** is made when you tie the ends of rope or cord together.

→ *He tied a **knot** in his shoelaces, so they wouldn't come off during the race.*

linguist [liŋgwist] *n.*

A **linguist** is someone who studies languages.

→ *Tony is a good **linguist** and speaks four different languages.*

participant [pɑ:rtísəpənt] *n.*

A **participant** is someone who joins in a social event or competition.

→ *There were thousands of **participants** in this year's marathon.*

plausible [plɔ́:zəbəl] *adj.*

If something is **plausible,** it is reasonable or possible.

→ *It is **plausible** that Jack isn't here today because he is sick.*

ritual [ritʃuəl] *n.*

A **ritual** is a formal custom that people do regularly.

→ *Ken was very interested to learn about the religious **rituals** of the natives.*

sibling [sibliŋ] *n.*

A ***sibling*** is a brother or sister.

→ *Jane has two **siblings,** an older brother and a younger sister.*

skinny [skini] *adj.*

If someone is **skinny**, they are extremely thin.

→ *Polly is very **skinny**. I think she needs to eat more.*

vague [veig] *adj.*

If something is **vague,** it is not clear, and it gives very few details.

→ *I asked him about his mother's health, but he was very **vague** about it.*

Exercise 1

Choose the answer that best fits the question.

1. Cosmetics are typically used to make someone ________.
   a. look better b. think clearer c. feel stronger d. eat healthier
2. Which of the following would NOT be considered a subject studied in humanities
   a. Film b. Literature c. Mythology d. Mathematics
3. Which of the following could NOT be used to make a knot?
   a. Lines of clouds b. Wire c. Thread d. Yarn
4. Positive attributes include being energetic, optimistic, and ________.
   a. dreary b. pessimistic c. cheerful d. arrogant
5. Which of the following is similar in meaning to the word dash?
   a. Stroll b. Run c. Sprint d. Meander

Exercise 2

Choose the one that is similar in meaning to the given word.

1. astounded
   a. angry b. surprised c. interested d. bored
2. disgust
   a. information b. detail c. money d. anger
3. gulf
   a. island b. gap c. entrance d. partnership
4. vague
   a. pretty b. useful c. unclear d. dirty
5. furious
   a. lively b. quiet c. angry d. shocking
6. bilingual
   a. foreign b. surprised c. poison d. using two languag
7. clone
   a. double b. extra c. light d. copy
8. plausible
   a. never b. always c. possible d. weak
9. skinny
   a. large b. thin c. tall d. short
10. fluorescent
    a. bright b. gloomy c. open d. ground

Exercise 3

Write C if the italicized word is used correctly. Write I if the word is used incorrectly.

1. ____ Kevin was very *vague* about his job interview, and he told me all the details.

2. ____ Liam had a *plausible* reason for not doing his work, saying aliens took it.

3. ____ Tom can only speak English. He is *bilingual.*

4. ____ Emma likes studying *humanities* like chemistry and physics.

5. ____ Ivy doesn't have any *siblings*. It must be lonely without brothers or sisters.

6. ____ The two brothers looked so much alike that they could be *clones*.

7. ____ My mother was *furious* when she heard that I passed all my exams.

8. ____ Miranda is so *skinny*. She really needs to lose some weight.

9. ____ I was filled with *disgust* when I heard the news that he had lied to all of us.

10. ____ Sarah and I really understand each other. There is a big *gulf* between us.

11. ____ Around the world, there are lots of different marriage *rituals*.

12. ____ We had lots of *participants* in the fishing competition last Saturday.

13. ____ Kay is a *linguist* and will give a lecture on the best way to learn a language.

14. ____ You should wear dark clothes for the interview, such as your *fluorescent* jacket.

15. ____ You always *dash* so slowly. I wish you would walk faster.

16. ____ I can't use this thread for sewing because it has too many *knots* in it.

17. ____ Jan wanted to make a cake, so she went to the shop to buy some *cosmetics*.

18. ____ The lesson was long and boring, and all the students felt *astounded*.

19. ____ I think Tom should get the job because he has all the right *attributes*.

20. ____ You shouldn't use *colloquial* language when you make formal presentations.

The Twins

Katie and Alice were twins. They were so alike that few people could tell the **siblings** apart. They were almost like **clones**. They even used the same **colloquial** language as each other. They were best friends.

But the twins' **attributes** were not all identical. Alice liked **humanities**, and Katie was a good **linguist**. One summer, Katie decided to be a **participant** at a summer camp in France. Alice wasn't interested in the French language, so she didn't go. But she felt angry that Katie wanted to spend the summer away from her.

Two months later, Katie returned. Alice **dashed** to the airport to greet her sister. But when Alice saw Katie, she was **astounded**. Katie was now **bilingual**, and she looked completely different! She was wearing nice clothes, **cosmetics** and looked **skinnier**. Alice felt very messy next to her. She was just wearing a **fluorescent** t-shirt, and her hair had **knots** in it.

When Alice asked Katie about France, Katie was **vague** and didn't say much. It made Alice **furious** and filled her with **disgust** because in the past they'd always told each other everything. Now there was a huge **gulf** between them. Over the weeks, the sisters spoke even less.

Two months later, it was the twins' birthday. All their lives, they'd had a **ritual**. Before their birthday, they'd talk all night long. That night, Alice came into Katie's bedroom.

"I'm sorry I haven't spoken much lately," Katie said.

"I understand. You have new friends now," said Alice, angrily.

Katie said, "My French friends don't write much nowadays. For a while, I thought they were more exciting than my friends at home. But I was wrong. You're my sister, and you'll always be my best friend."

Alice said, "I'm sorry, too. I wanted our relationship to stay the same forever. But it's totally **plausible** for twins to have different interests. We can still be best friends without being together all the time."

Reading Comprehension

PART A Mark each statement T for true or F for false. Rewrite the false statements to make them true.

1. ____ The girls looked like clones, but they used different colloquial language.

   ____

2. ____ The twins' attributes were different in that Katie was bilingual and Alice liked humanities.

   ____

3. ____ Alice's hair was in knots when she dashed to the airport to meet her sister.

   ____

4. ____ Alice was astounded when she saw Katie wearing a fluorescent t-shirt.

   ____

5. ____ When the gulf formed between the sisters, they stopped speaking to each other in detail.

   ____

PART B Answer the questions.

1. Why didn't Alice want to be a participant at the summer camps with the other linguists?

   ____

   ____

2. How did Alice feel when she saw Katie looking skinny and wearing cosmetics?

   ____

   ____

3. Why was Alice furious and filled with disgust when Katie answered her questions in a vague way?

   ____

   ____

4. What ritual did the siblings always do before their birthday?

   ____

   ____

5. What did Alice learn was plausible?

   ____

   ____

UNIT 22

Word List

acid [ǽsid] *n.*

An **acid** is a chemical that can burn or dissolve other substances.
→ *In chemistry class, we mixed two **acids** together and watched the reaction.*

administration [ədminəstréiʃən] *n.*

An **administration** is the group of people who manage a company or organization.
→ *She hoped she could be promoted to a job in the **administration**.*

administrative [ədmínəstrèitiv] *adj.*

Administrative describes anything related to managing a company or organization.
→ *I work as an **administrative** assistant to the owner of the company.*

biotechnology [bàiouteknáləd͡ʒi] *n.*

Biotechnology is the use of living parts, such as cells, in industry and technology.
→ *Researchers at the **biotechnology** company use bacteria to make medicine.*

cholesterol [kəléstəroul] *n.*

Cholesterol is a substance in fat, tissues, and blood of all animals.
→ *When people have too much **cholesterol**, they are at a high risk for heart problems.*

coalition [kòuəliʃən] *n.*

A **coalition** is a group of people or organizations working for a common purpose.
→ *The companies formed a **coalition** to make trade less expensive.*

deceptive [diséptiv] *adj.*

When something is **deceptive**, it encourages one to believe something that is false.
→ *The scary-looking man's appearance is **deceptive**, but he is actually very nice.*

diabetes [dàiəbí:tis] *n.*

Diabetes is a medical condition where a person has too much sugar in their blood.
→ *Overweight people are more likely to suffer from **diabetes** than slimmer ones.*

eliminate [ilímənèit] *v.*

To **eliminate** something that is unwanted means to completely remove it.
→ *Wearing a seatbelt **eliminates** some of the dangers of driving a car.*

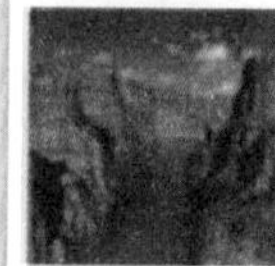

erosion [iróuʒən] *n.*

Erosion is the destruction of rock or soil due to flowing water or weather.
→ *Canyons are formed because rivers of fast-moving water caused **erosion**.*

ethics [eθiks] *n.*

Ethics are moral beliefs or rules about right or wrong.
→ *The act of stealing certainly doesn't go against some people's* ***ethics.***

explicit [iksplisit] *adj.*

If something is **explicit,** it is very clear, open, and truthful.
→ *The man gave a very* ***explicit*** *account of the car accident.*

framework [fréimwə̀:rk] *n.*

A **framework** is a set of rules or ideas that people use to solve problems.
→ *His ideas fit into the* ***framework*** *of a successful business plan.*

manufacture [mæ̀njəfǽktʃə:r] *v.*

To **manufacture** something means to make it in a factory.
→ *My father's company* ***manufactures*** *steel building materials.*

mechanism [mékənizəm] *n.*

A **mechanism** is a part of a machine that performs a certain function.
→ *I can't open my car door because the locking* ***mechanism*** *is broke.*

minimize [minəmàiz] *v.*

To **minimize** means to reduce something to the lowest possible level.
→ *I checked my homework twice to* ***minimize*** *errors I might have made.*

nectar [néktər] *n.*

Nectar is a sweet liquid produced by flowers that bees and other insects collect.
→ *Bees use* ***nectar*** *to make their honey.*

notion [nóuʃən] *n.*

A **notion** is an idea or belief about something.
→ *I have a* ***notion*** *that this route would get us to the beach.*

prone [proun] *adj.*

When things are **prone** to some bad thing, they are likely affected by it.
→ *Some people are more* ***prone*** *to catching colds than others.*

straightforward [strèitfɔ́:rwərd] *adj.*

When something is **straightforward,** it is good because it is easy to understand.
→ *The teacher's grading system was* ***straightforward*** *and fair.*

Exercise 1

Choose the answer that best fits the question.

1. What is something you want to eliminate?
   a. A problem
   b. A present
   c. A statue
   d. A victory

2. What would collect nectar?
   a. A tree
   b. A bee
   c. A cat
   d. A housefly

3. If you have good ethics, you _______.
   a. dislike school
   b. know right from wrong
   c. rarely follow the rules
   d. are extremely smart

4. Which is most closely related to something administrative?
   a. Loss
   b. Fatigue
   c. Organization
   d. Swimming

5. What might cause erosion?
   a. A strong wind
   b. A fast car
   c. A lonely person
   d. Loud music

Exercise 2

Fill in the blanks with the correct words from the word bank.

Word Bank

cholesterol	prone	framework	administration	explicit
deceptive	coalition	mechanisms	straightforward	manufactures

I learned about all the different things the factory 1_____________.
They make big machinery as well as tiny parts and 2_____________.

The students asked the school's 3_____________ to buy a better kind of meat.
The meat served there is too high in fat and 4_____________.

I can't stand companies that are 5_____________.
Customers have to make sure they get 6_____________ information about all details.

Citizens formed a 7_____________ because the city's air was making people ill.
Elderly people and infants were the most 8_____________ to becoming sick.

To solve our problem, we'll first need a strong 9_____________.
Our ideas need to be intelligent and 10_____________.

Exercise 3

Write C if the italicized word is used correctly. Write I if the word is used incorrectly.

1. ____ Smoking makes people more *prone* to breathing problems.

2. ____ We toured the factory that *manufactures* cheese.

3. ____ The *deceptive* man was very open and honest about his plans.

4. ____ Eating a lot of fast food raises people's *cholesterol* levels.

5. ____ The *straightforward* instructions were impossible to understand.

6. ____ The group decided on a *framework* for the new project.

7. ____ Businesses try to *minimize* the amount of money they can make.

8. ____ He had a *notion* that the speaker was not really an expert on the subject.

9. ____ The maid used a kind of *acid* to dissolve the stains on the floor.

10. ____ It is important for a judge to have good *ethics*.

11. ____ Some factories produce energy by burning *coalitions*.

12. ____ The lawyer hoped that the witness would tell an *explicit* version of the story.

13. ____ My father works in construction while my mom has an *administrative* job.

14. ____ Be sure to *eliminate* all the ingredients to make a great cake.

15. ____ Jim receives shots to treat his *diabetes*. They reduce the sugar in his blood.

16. ____ All of the prisoners formed an *administration* where they played games.

17. ____ Dry weather, followed by sudden floods, caused the *erosion* in the valley.

18. ____ The *biotechnology* company only made things from nonliving rocks and sand.

19. ____ The cutting *mechanism* on the lawnmower is broken.

20. ____ This *nectar* produces the best flowers.

The New Bioco

Jack got a new job at a **biotechnology** company called Bioco. Bioco **manufactured** drugs to treat **diabetes** and high **cholesterol**. Jack's job was to use a tiny **mechanism** to get **nectar** from flowers. The nectar was a main ingredient in the drugs. Jack liked his job, and he thought that Bioco was a caring company. However, Jack soon learned that the company wasn't as kind as he first thought.

Bioco's motto was "Make the Earth a Better Place." However, this motto was **deceptive**. The company actually did a number of really bad things to the environment. The company produced a lot of smog and harmful **acid**. Bioco poured the acid in a nearby river, which caused **erosion** and made fish **prone** to illness.

After a few weeks at the new job, Jack saw all the bad things Bioco was doing. He had always had strong **ethics**, and he knew he had to do something. One day, while the Bioco workers were eating in the cafeteria, Jack stood up and gave a speech. He said, "My fellow coworkers, I know you have all seen the evil things our company is doing. I have a **notion** that we can fix them if we form a **coalition**. We can go to the **administration** and tell them we'll quit if they don't **eliminate** the problems. They'll have no choice but to listen to us."

Jack explained what they were to do. His coworkers liked his **explicit** plan. They went to the **administrative** offices and demanded that Bioco stop damaging the environment, or they all would quit. One supervisor said to them, "Thank you for being **straightforward** about this issue. Since I can't afford to lose all of you workers, I guess we'll just have to fix things."

Jack, his supervisor, and his coworkers spent the next month designing a new **framework** for the company. They cleaned up the acid from the river and **minimized** the amount of air pollution the company released. At last, the company motto became apt.

Reading Comprehension

PART A Mark each statement T for true or F for false. Rewrite the false statements to make them true.

1. ____ Bioco was a biotechnology company that manufactured diabetes and high cholesterol.

____

2. ____ Jack used a mechanism to get nectar from flowers.

____

3. ____ The new framework involved an explicit plan to fix the smog and acid problems.

____

4. ____ The waste acid caused erosion and made fish prone to illness.

____

5. ____ After the company minimized Jack's ethics, the motto became apt.

____

PART B Answer the questions.

1. What was Bioco's deceptive motto?

____

____

2. What did Jack stand up to do in the cafeteria?

____

____

3. What was Jack's notion about fixing things?

____

____

4. What did the coalition of workers threaten to do if the administration didn't eliminate the problems?

____

____

5. What did the boss in the offices say after the workers were straightforward with him?

____

____

UNIT 23

Word List

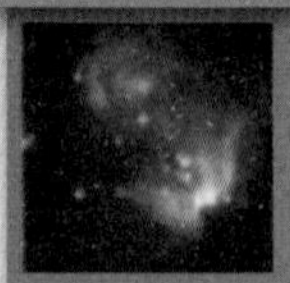

astronomical [æstrənάmikkəl] *adj.*

If something is **astronomical**, then it is extremely large.

→ *It's an **astronomical** distance between the Milky Way galaxy and the nearest galaxy.*

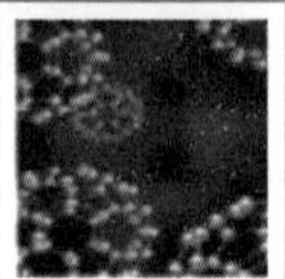

atom [ǽtəm] *n.*

An **atom** is the smallest unit of a substance.

→ *A molecule consists of a combination of two or more **atoms**.*

breadth [bredə] *n.*

Breadth is the distance from one side to the other side of something.

→ *The **breadth** of the northern wall of the house is twenty meters.*

circumference [sərkʌ́mfərəns] *n.*

A **circumference** is the distance completely around a circular object.

→ *The **circumference** of the Earth is obviously much larger than a baseball's.*

comet [kάmit] *n.*

A **comet** is an object in space made of ice and rock with a tail of glowing dust.

→ ***Comets** take many decades to complete an orbit around a star.*

crater [kréitər] *n.*

A **crater** is a large hole in a planet's or moon's surface.

→ *They could clearly see the big **crater** on the moon through the telescope.*

crescent [krésənt] *n.*

A **crescent** is the curved shape lit on the moon's face during its early and late stages

→ *Ten days ago the entire moon was bright, but now only a small **crescent** is shining*

debris [dəbri:] *n.*

Debris is the small pieces scattered from something wrecked or destroyed.

→ *The **debris** from the cube scattered on the floor.*

despair [dispɛ́ər] *n.*

Despair is the complete loss of hope.

→ *After the other company won the account, our salespeople were filled with **despa***

embed [imbéd] *v.*

To **embed** something means to place it firmly within a surrounding thing.

→ *The logger **embedded** the ax into the wood after chopping several logs.*

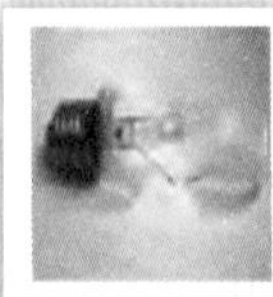

fragment [frægmənt] *n.*

A **fragment** is a small part of something.

→ *After the light broke, there were **fragments** of glass to clean up.*

galaxy [gæləksi] *n.*

A **galaxy** is any extremely large collection of star systems.

→ *Our solar system is located in the outer area of our **galaxy**.*

gigantic [dʒaigæntik] *adj.*

If something is **gigantic**, then it is extremely large.

→ *Some dinosaurs were so **gigantic** that they were the size of buildings.*

gloom [glu:m] *n.*

Gloom is a state of being almost completely dark.

→ *In the **gloom** of the morning, it was difficult to see the boat on the lake.*

radiate [rèidièit] *v.*

To **radiate** means to send out energy or heat.

→ *The heat from the fireplace **radiated** throughout the room.*

roam [roum] *v.*

To **roam** means to move around without a plan or purpose.

→ *All day the cows **roamed** around the field eating grass.*

solitary [sάlitèri] *adj.*

If something is **solitary**, then it is lonely or the only one.

→ *The only thing in the room was a **solitary** chair.*

spectrum [spèktrəm] *n.*

The ***spectrum*** is the full range of color ranging from red to violet.

→ *You can see the entire **spectrum** in a rainbow.*

sphere [sfiə:r] *n.*

A **sphere** is a three-dimensional round shape, like a ball.

→ *The balloons were inflated into a variety of colorful **spheres**.*

status [steitəs] *n.*

Status is the position of something or someone in relation to others.

→ *She had achieved the **status** of being the smartest girl in the class.*

Exercise 1

Choose the one that is similar in meaning to the given word.

1. radiate
   a. measure b. release c. welcome d. allow
2. breadth
   a. path b. death c. mouth d. width
3. spectrum
   a. colors b. amounts c. sounds d. places
4. comet
   a. arrival b. meteor c. scissors d. image
5. atom
   a. particle b. catch c. fast d. legal
6. status
   a. land b. rock c. rank d. cloud
7. astronomical
   a. historical b. pleasant c. delicious d. huge
8. embed
   a. sleep b. soften c. bury d. burn
9. sphere
   a. tide b. voice c. mass d. ball
10. debris
    a. pieces b. troops c. cloths d. liquids

Exercise 2

Choose the one that is opposite in meaning to the given word.

1. crater
   a. basket b. habit c. spouse d. hill
2. gloom
   a. plan b. book c. light d. hole
3. solitary
   a. chain b. group c. home d. card
4. gigantic
   a. wild b. tiny c. next d. free
5. roam
   a. buy b. break c. get d. stand
6. fragment
   a. whole b. child c. phone d. point
7. despair
   a. burn b. hope c. sing d. make
8. galaxy
   a. delivery b. marriage c. particle d. agreement
9. crescent
   a. circle b. closet c. problem d. schedule
10. circumference
    a. feeling b. detail c. center d. helmet

Exercise 3

Choose the answer that best fits the question.

1. What is something that is astronomical?
   a. A planet b. A book c. An ant d. A movie
2. What is something you'd find in a galaxy?
   a. A pear b. A broom c. A star d. A motorcycle
3. Which would help you see through the gloom of a day?
   a. Glasses b. A telescope c. A candle d. A cap
4. Which of the following is a sphere?
   a. A globe b. A bat c. A golf club d. A television set
5. What describes someone whose waist has a large circumference?
   a. Tall b. Fat c. Strong d. Skinny

Exercise 4

Write a word that is similar in meaning to the underlined part.

1. The night was extremely dark because little light came from the curved shaped moon.
   ____
2. They moved without a purpose around the mall while waiting for their friend to get off of work.
   ____
3. The moon has large holes on the surface.
   ____
4. The distance from one side to the other of a baby's hand is very small.
   ____
5. Mom couldn't fix the bowl because a small part of it was missing.
   ____
6. A lot of energy is stored within just one simple smallest unit of matter.
   ____
7. The bee's stinger was placed firmly within the skin of his right hand.
   ____
8. Guarding the camp was a lonely job, so he gladly accepted the young man's company.
   ____
9. When it's low on fuel, the heater emits a small level of heat.
   ____
10. He was so concerned about his position to others in school that he studied very hard.
   ____

How Comet Got His Tail

A **solitary** rock **roamed** through the cold **gloom** of outer space. It slowly drifted through the **debris** of broken asteroids with a feeling of sadness. In the vast and beautiful **galaxy,** it was only a tiny rock. It felt like an insignificant **atom**.

In its journeys it encountered many amazing objects. It flew by beautiful **crescent** moons that were covered with **craters** and moon dust.

"Why can't I be as beautiful as them?" it thought.

The rock passed a **gigantic** planet. The **sphere** had a **circumference** hundreds of times larger than the **breadth** of the small rock.

"Why can't I be as large as that?" it wondered.

The rock was filled with **despair**. It was surrounded by beauty and greatness, yet it was just a small and ugly **fragment** of rock.

One day, it approached the area of an **astronomical** star.

"What's wrong?" the star asked.

"Oh, I wish I had a higher **status** in the galaxy. All the other objects are so beautiful and large," the rock replied. "But I'm just an ugly rock."

The star considered the problem. At last it said, "You don't have to worry anymore. I think I can help." The star **radiated** its light brighter and hotter than it had ever done before. "Come a little closer," the star said to the rock.

The rock drifted closer to the star. Suddenly, the ice that was **embedded** in the rock's tiny cracks melted and became steam. Then the steam extended behind the comet to form a brilliant tail. The tail shined with all the colors of the **spectrum**.

The little rock had become a beautiful **comet**. It looked so amazing. It realized that the star helped it change its appearance. "Thank you," the comet said and then flew away with its new beautiful tail following behind it like a galactic cape.

Reading Comprehension

PART A Mark each statement T for true or F for false. Rewrite the false statements to make them true.

1. ____ The little rock drifted through the debris of broken atoms.

2. ____ The gigantic planet was in the shape of a sphere.

3. ____ The ice embedded in the little rock bubbled with all the colors of the spectrum.

4. ____ The star radiated its light hotter and brighter than ever before.

5. ____ The little rock wished it had a higher status in the galaxy.

PART B Answer the questions.

1. While roaming through the gloom of the galaxy, how did the little rock feel?

2. What objects had craters and was in the shape of a shiny crescent?

3. How much larger was the circumference of the planet compared to the breadth of the rock?

4. Why was the little fragment of rock filled with despair?

5. What did the comet's new tail look like?

UNIT 24

Word List

bankrupt [bǽŋkrʌpt] *adj.*

If someone is **bankrupt**, then they are unable to pay their debts.

→ *The store had few customers and soon went **bankrupt**.*

conform [kənfɔ́ːrm] *v.*

To **conform** to rules or laws is to obey them.

→ *The new student had to **conform** to the school's dress code.*

employ [implɔ́i] *v.*

To **employ** someone means to give work to them.

→ *The bookstore **employed** two full-time clerks.*

expel [ikspél] *v.*

To **expel** someone means to force them to leave a place.

→ *Since he would not follow the rules, the principal had to **expel** the student.*

extension [iksténʃən] *n.*

An **extension** is a part added to something to give it more time or space.

→ *My parents decided to add an **extension** to our house for the new baby.*

forthcoming [fɔ̀ːrθkʌ́miŋ] *adj.*

If something is **forthcoming**, then it is about to happen in the future.

→ *Some economists predicted that the **forthcoming** world economy would be severe.*

furnish [fə́ːrniʃ] *v.*

To furnish means to put **furniture** in a house or room.

→ *Most homes are **furnished** with tables, chairs, and beds.*

hygiene [háidʒiːn] *n.*

Hygiene is the conditions or methods needed for health and cleanliness.

→ *People who brush their teeth at least twice a day are practicing good **hygiene**.*

hygienic [haidʒíːnik] *adj.*

If something is **hygienic**, then it is clean and unlikely to cause disease.

→ *My sister works very hard to keep her entire home as **hygienic** as possible.*

landlord [lǽndlɔ̀ːrd] *n.*

A **landlord** is a man who rents property to a person.

→ *The **landlord** collected everyone's rent money on the first day of every month.*

lease [li:s] *v.*

To **lease** means to rent property, usually an apartment or land.

→ *When the family first **leased** the apartment, the rent was very low.*

mandatory [mændətɔ:ri] *adj.*

If something is **mandatory**, then it is required by law.

→ *It's **mandatory** that everyone be at least sixteen to drive a car in the US.*

mend [mend] *v.*

To **mend** something means to fix it when it is broken or damaged.

→ *Mother **mended** the rip in my pants with a piece of cloth.*

mortgage [mɔ́:rgidʒ] *n.*

A **mortgage** is a loan for property, especially homes and businesses.

→ *When they bought their new home, the married couple had to sign a **mortgage**.*

personnel [pə̀:rsənél] *n.*

Personnel are employees in a business.

→ *When business increased, we had to hire more **personnel**.*

plumbing [plʌ́miŋ] *n.*

Plumbing is the system of pipes used in a home to supply water.

→ *When the **plumbing** stopped working, no one was allowed to use the toilets.*

tenant [tenənt] *n.*

A **tenant** is a person who rents property from a landlord.

→ *The new **tenants** moved into the house across the street.*

trendy [tréndi] *adj.*

If something is **trendy**, then it is very popular and new.

→ *Carlo bought a **trendy** new car.*

utility [ju:tíləti] *n.*

A **utility** is a business that supplies services such as water or electricity.

→ *If you don't pay the **utilities**, you may have your electricity turned off.*

whereby [hwɛə:rbai] *conj.*

Whereby means by which or through which.

→ *The mayor had a new bridge built **whereby** the citizens could cross the river.*

Exercise 1

Choose the answer that best fits the question.

1. Which of the following means the closest to mend?
   a. Repair b. Highlight c. Exchange d. Plant
2. Which of following would NOT be considered part of an office's personnel?
   a. Cleaning staff b. Technicians c. Executives d. Referees
3. Plumbing involves work on ________ in a house or building.
   a. electrical wiring b. plants and bushes c. water pipes d. interior design
4. If something is trendy, then it is ________.
   a. outdated b. in style c. almost empty d. very cheap
5. Which is NOT considered a utility?
   a. Room service b. Electrical service c. Water service d. Gas service

Exercise 2

Write a word that is similar in meaning to the underlined part.

1. His company <u>gives work to</u> about 100 people in the community.

   ____

2. Joan was <u>forced to leave</u> from the auditorium for her hostile comments.

   ____

3. My new apartment in the city was <u>complete with bed, sofa, and TV</u>.

   ____

4. The prisoner's <u>condition for health and cleanliness</u> was absolutely terrible.

   ____

5. I'm going to <u>rent</u> the apartment for only six months.

   ____

6. I need to <u>fix</u> the hole in my pants.

   ____

7. He was lucky to find <u>employees</u> who are honest and hardworking.

   ____

8. We need to have our <u>system of pipes that brings water into our house</u> checked.

   ____

9. The <u>popular and new</u> fashion these days for men is boots.

   ____

10. Did you remember to pay the <u>company that provides our water</u>?

   ____

Exercise 3

Write C if the italicized word is used correctly. Write I if the word is used incorrectly.

1. ____ The sharp rocks *mended* his jeans into pieces.
2. ____ The school sent a second bus *whereby* the students could get to school.
3. ____ He had poor *hygiene*. He never washed his hands or brushed his teeth.
4. ____ The dam on the lake became *bankrupt*, and soon water broke through the cracks.
5. ____ The restaurant was a *trendy* place where all the rich and famous people went.
6. ____ The first three cars to finish were given an award, but the *forthcoming* car got nothing.
7. ____ She made a mistake and accidentally walked into the *mandatory* bathroom.
8. ____ After he *furnished* dinner, the host gave him some dessert.
9. ____ Rather than *conforming* to one religion, Mary chose what she liked from all of them.
10. ____ I knew something was wrong with the *plumbing* once the hot water stopped working.
11. ____ She graduated from university where she studied *utility*.
12. ____ Because of an error, the game was given an *extension* of five more minutes.
13. ____ He's very *hygienic* because he bathes once a week and seldom changes his clothes.
14. ____ The *landlord* owned several buildings throughout the capital city.
15. ____ The factory needed more workers. It had to *employ* twenty more people.
16. ____ Tom didn't want to talk about his father's new job. He thought it was too *personnel*.
17. ____ There was too much sugar in the recipe, so she *leased* the amount with a spoon.
18. ____ Because the rent was so expensive, all of the *tenants* are probably wealthy people.
19. ____ They were *expelled* from the restaurant because they couldn't pay their bill.
20. ____ In order to buy a house, most people have to get a *mortgage*.

The Resourceful Landlord

A kind **landlord** was afraid that he would lose his apartment building. He needed to make some **mandatory** repairs to the old building, or his **tenants** would have to leave by the end of the month. Without tenants to **lease** the rooms, the landlord would be unable to pay his **mortgage**. He'd be **bankrupt**, and the bank would take his building.

But he didn't have the money **whereby** he could **employ** the **personnel** needed to make the repairs. It would seem like he did not want to **conform** to the city's codes before the **forthcoming** inspection. He had requested an **extension**, but it was denied by the city.

He held a meeting with his tenants and explained the unfortunate situation. "If the building does not meet the appropriate standards for safety and **hygiene**," he said, "the city will **expel** everyone."

The tenants were all sad for the kind old man.

"Maybe we can help," the hairdresser who lived on the first floor stated. The other tenants agreed.

One tenant had worked for the city's **utilities**. He knew a lot about **plumbing**, so that's how he helped. Another tenant was a carpenter; he **mended** the holes in the floor and walls. Others cleaned the building from top to bottom so that it was more **hygienic**. They even **furnished** some of the apartments with new beds, dressers, and chairs. When they were done, all of the people dispersed, and the landlord went home to rest.

When the deadline of the inspection arrived, the apartment building was hygienic and safe. The landlord couldn't believe it. His old building now looked like one of the **trendiest** buildings in town. The building passed its inspection, and the landlord and the tenants had a big party.

"Thank you all so much," the landlord said during the party. "I could never have done it by myself. But by working together, we now all have a beautiful place to live."

Reading Comprehension

PART A Mark each statement T for true or F for false. Rewrite the false statements to make them true.

1. ____ If the tenants didn't pay the mortgage, the landlord could not pay his lease and would be bankrupt.

   ____

2. ____ The landlord did not have money whereby he could employ personnel.

   ____

3. ____ The city would expel everyone if the building did not pass the inspection for safety and hygiene.

   ____

4. ____ The hairdresser mended the holes in the floors and walls.

   ____

5. ____ After everyone helped to fix it, the building looked like one of the trendiest buildings in town.

   ____

PART B Answer the questions.

1. In addition to dressers, what did the tenants furnish some of the apartments with?

   ____

   ____

2. If the landlord did not conform to the city's mandatory hygienic standards, what would happen to the tenants?

   ____

   ____

3. What happened to the landlord's request for an extension to the forthcoming deadline?

   ____

   ____

4. What did the tenant who had worked for the city's utilities do to the building's plumbing?

   ____

   ____

5. What did the landlord do after all of the people dispersed?

   ____

   ____

UNIT 25

Word List

aesthetic [əseétik] *adj.*

If something is **aesthetic**, then it is concerned with a love of beauty.

→ *The dresses were noteworthy for their **aesthetic** design.*

arrogant [ǽrəgənt] *adj.*

If someone is **arrogant**, they think that they are more important than others.

→ *He is very **arrogant**. Even though he's not the boss, he tells everyone what to do.*

bias [báiəs] *n.*

A **bias** is a person's likelihood to like one thing more than another thing.

→ *The mothers had a natural **bias** for their own child's picture.*

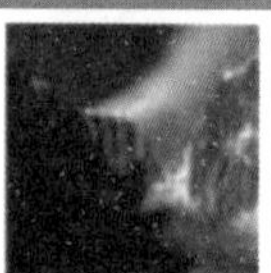

canyon [kǽnjən] *n.*

A **canyon** is a narrow valley with steep walls through which a river often flows.

→ *The **canyon** was so deep that the ground inside was covered in shadow.*

creek [kri:k] *n.*

A **creek** is a stream or small river.

→ *Only small fish lived in the shallow waters of the **creek**.*

drill [dril] *n.*

A **drill** is a tool with a point that spins in order to make a hole.

→ *The carpenter used the **drill** to make several holes in the wood.*

executive [igzékjətiv] *n.*

An **executive** is the top manager of a business.

→ *After twenty years at the company, he finally became the **executive**.*

fatigue [fəti:g] *n.*

Fatigue is a feeling of extreme tiredness.

→ *After three days with little sleep, she was feeling a lot of **fatigue**.*

incline [ínklain] *n.*

An **incline** is a sharp rise in something, especially a hill or mountain.

→ *This mountain has one of the steepest **inclines** in the world.*

nasty [nǽsti] *adj.*

If something is **nasty**, then it is not nice or pleasant.

→ *The rotten apple left a **nasty** taste inside her mouth.*

perceive [pərsíːv] *v.*

To **perceive** something means to be aware of it.

→ *He was talking loudly, so he did not* ***perceive*** *that the music had stopped.*

primate [práimeit] *n.*

A **primate** is a type of mammal that includes monkeys, apes, and humans.

→ ***Primates*** *use their hands for such tasks as swinging from branches.*

primitive [prímətiv] *adj.*

If something is **primitive**, then it is simple, basic, and not very developed.

→ *The computers of the 1980s are* ***primitive*** *compared to those of todays.*

stereotype [stériətàip] *n.*

A **stereotype** is a general but often incorrect idea about a person or thing.

→ *There's a* ***stereotype*** *that pigs are dirty animals. But they are rather clean.*

sticky [stíki] *adj.*

If something is **sticky**, then it is covered with a substance that things stick to.

→ *Place the* ***sticky*** *part of the tape against the paper, so it will cling to the wall.*

termite [tə́ːrmait] *n.*

A **termite** is an insect that lives in groups and feeds on wood.

→ *The wood we found was full of* ***termites****.*

thereby [ðὲəːrbái] *adv.*

If something happens **thereby** an action, then it is the result of that action.

→ *He didn't score a goal,* ***thereby*** *ending his chance at setting a record.*

trail [treil] *n.*

A **trail** is a path through a wild area.

→ *A narrow* ***trail*** *cut through the field and over the hills.*

twig [twig] *n.*

A **twig** is a short and thin branch from a tree or bush.

→ *They started the fire with a handful of dry* ***twigs****.*

welfare [wélfὲəːr] *n.*

Welfare is the health and happiness of a person or group.

→ *Having plenty of clean water is necessary for the* ***welfare*** *of people.*

Exercise 1

Choose the answer that best fits the question.

1. Which of the following might be eaten by a termite?
   a. A log b. A brick
   c. A cake d. A feather

2. Who would most likely use a drill?
   a. A captain b. A carpenter
   c. A cowboy d. A lifeguard

3. What job would an executive do?
   a. Clean floors b. Manage workers
   c. Teach science d. Prepare food

4. What would best describe something that smells nasty?
   a. Sweet b. Steamy
   c. Stinky d. Pleasant

5. How would you describe someone who could NOT perceive sound?
   a. Deaf b. Blind
   c. Quiet d. Mute

Exercise 2

Fill in the blanks with the correct words from the word bank.

Word Bank

trail	stereotype	twig	canyon	creek
fatigue	aesthetic	welfare	primitive	termites

The path leading out of the 1_______________ was very steep.
When they reached the top, they had to rest because of their 2_______________.

He had a(n) 3_______________ about ancient cultures.
He thought that all their customs and ideas were 4_______________.

The 5_______________ led travelers to the top of the mountain.
I was astonished by the 6_______________ view.

A line of 7_______________ stretched from the mound across the forest floor.
They were all going to eat a 8_______________ that had fallen off a tree.

People thought that the water from the 9_______________ cured illnesses.
They drank it because they hoped it would beneficial to their 10_______________.

Exercise 3

Choose the one that is similar in meaning to the given word.

1. perceive
   a. notice b. share c. copy d. gain
2. welfare
   a. welcome b blanket c. health d. sale
3. bias
   a. herb b. sock c. box d. favoritism
4. arrogant
   a. proud b. bright c. loose d. loud
5. creek
   a. button b. truck c. stream d. arrow
6. nasty
   a. slow b. small c. smooth d. mean
7. executive
   a. group b. boss c. monster d. finger
8. trail
   a. path b. moment c. song d. mirror
9. incline
   a. rise b. cotton c. shoulder d. soldier
10. thereby
    a. growth b. section c. dream d. so

Exercise 4

Write a word that is similar in meaning to the underlined part.

1. The kids gathered <u>short, thing branches</u> for their school art project.

   ____

2. The glue was <u>covered with a substance that made things stick to it</u>.

   ____

3. Early rocket development was <u>simple and basic</u> compared to what we have in the 21st century.

   ____

4. <u>Monkeys, apes, and humans</u> are some of the few animals with opposable thumbs.

   ____

5. After walking 12 kilometers, I was filled with a sense of <u>extreme tiredness</u>.

   ____

The Man and the Monkey

While flying over a jungle, a wealthy **executive**'s private plane crashed. Some of the crew were hurt, so the pilot decided to stay with them and wait for help. The **arrogant** executive, though, didn't care about the **welfare** of the pilot and crew. Rather, he thought he could walk out of the jungle and find a town to stay in.

He followed a **trail** through a **canyon** and along a **creek**. The jungle was actually very stunning. If the arrogant executive had stopped to look around, he might have **perceived** the jungle's beauty. But he was in a **nasty** mood and had no care for the **aesthetic** value of the jungle. He continued to walk up the steep **incline** of the jungle's hills.

Soon, he was lost. Several days passed, and **fatigue** and hunger weakened him. He was very tired and afraid.

Just then, a monkey came out of the trees. It was carrying a **twig** covered in honey. It walked up to a mound where **termites** lived. He then used the twig like a **drill** to make a hole in the mound. Then very carefully, it removed the twig from the hole. The **sticky** twig was covered with termites.

Instead of eating the bugs, the monkey offered them to the executive, but he didn't want what the monkey offered. He shouted at the monkey, "Get away from me, you stupid **primate**!"

The executive's **stereotype** of the monkey was wrong. The monkey was not stupid. It knew how to find food, whereas the executive did not. He refused the help of the monkey, **thereby** leaving himself to starve.

When the executive was finally found, he was very skinny and sick. He had not eaten for a very long time. Because he held a **bias** against the **primitive** ways of the monkey, he had gone hungry and almost died. The executive didn't understand that it was his arrogant attitude that had caused all of his problems.

Reading Comprehension

PART A Mark each statement T for true or F for false. Rewrite the false statements to make them true.

1. ____ The executive only cared about the welfare of his pilot and crew.

____

2. ____ The executive followed a trail through a canyon and along a creek.

____

3. ____ The executive was in a nasty mood, so he did not see the aesthetic value of the jungle.

____

4. ____ The executive walked up the small incline of the jungle's hills.

____

5. ____ The executive's stereotype of the primate was correct.

____

PART B Answer the questions.

1. What was on the twig that made it sticky enough to capture termites?

____

____

2. What did hunger and fatigue do to the executive?

____

____

3. What happened to the executive because of his bias against the monkey's primitive ways?

____

____

4. What did the monkey use like it was a drill?

____

____

5. What did the executive never perceive about his arrogant attitude?

____

____

UNIT 26

Word List

behalf [bihǽf] *n.*

If something is done on one's **behalf**, it is done for that person by another.

→ *The original speaker was sick, so his son gave the speech on his **behalf**.*

flap [flæp] *v.*

To **flap** means to move quickly up and down or from side to side.

→ *The tiny bird **flapped** its wings and ate from the flowers.*

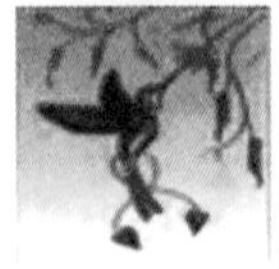

glacier [gléiʃər] *n.*

A **glacier** is a large piece of ice that moves very slowly.

→ *The North Pole is covered by a huge **glacier**.*

globe [gloub] *n.*

The **globe** refers to the Earth.

→ *Water covers most of the **globe**.*

horizontal [hɔ̀:rəzɑ́ntl] *adj.*

When something is **horizontal**, it is flat and level with the ground.

→ *The Russian flag has three **horizontal** stripes of white, blue, and red.*

hum [hʌm] *v.*

To **hum** means to make a low, continuous noise.

→ *The man **hummed** his favorite song.*

inventory [ínvəntɔ̀:ri] *n.*

An **inventory** is a supply of something.

→ *Gwen was checking the **inventory** to make sure we had what we needed.*

inward [inwərd] *adj.*

If a thought or feeling is **inward**, it is not expressed or shown to others.

→ *She had an **inward** feeling of guilt when she lied to her mother.*

loaf [louf] *n.*

A **loaf** of bread is bread shaped and baked in one piece.

→ *Could you please buy a **loaf** of bread for sandwiches?*

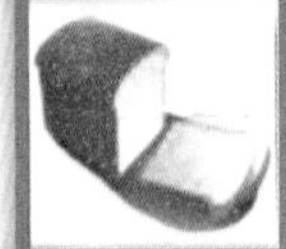

oracle [ɔ́(:)rəkəl] *n.*

An **oracle** is person who speaks with gods and gives advice about the future

→ *The king went to the **oracle** to ask if going to war was a good idea.*

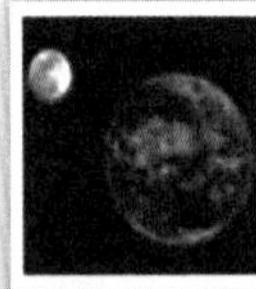

orbit [ɔ́:rbit] *v.*

To **orbit** something means to move around it in a continuous, curving path.

→ *The moon **orbits** the Earth.*

overview [óuvərvjùː] *n.*

An **overview** is a general description of a situation.

→ *My brother gave me an **overview** of the important parts of the book.*

preview [príːvjùː] *n.*

A **preview** is an opportunity to see something before it is available to the public.

→ *The band played us a **preview** of their new song.*

previous [príːviəs] *adj.*

If something is **previous**, then it happened earlier in time or order.

→ *He turned back to the **previous** page to read the paragraph again.*

provide [prəváid] *v.*

To **provide** something means to supply it.

→ *Each student was **provided** with a test and three sharp pencils.*

recur [rikə́ːr] *v.*

To **recur** means to happen more than once.

→ *Burglaries seem to **recur** over and over in our neighborhood.*

relevant [réləvənt] *adj.*

When something is **relevant**, it is important to a certain person or situation.

→ *The thirty-year-old book about politics is still **relevant** to our society today.*

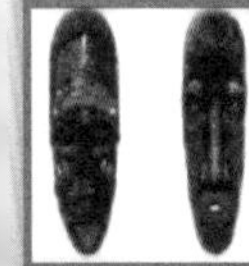

rite [rait] *n.*

A **rite** is a traditional ceremony carried out by a particular group or society.

→ *Special masks are worn during the **rite** when a new baby is born.*

stall [stɔːl] *v.*

To **stall** means to stop a process and continue it at a later time.

→ *If you give the car a push, it won't **stall**.*

supernatural [sùːpərnǽtʃərəl] *adj.*

If something is **supernatural**, it is not real or explainable by natural law.

→ *The dragon had **supernatural** powers such as flying and breathing fire.*

Exercise 1

Choose the answer that best fits the question.

1. What recurs when watching a funny movie?
a. Boredom
b. Laughter
c. Headaches
d. Hunger

2. What orbits the Earth?
a. The moon
b. A car
c. A bird
d. A kite

3. Why do birds flap their wings?
a. To eat
b. To fly
c. To whistle
d. To exercise

4. What is supernatural?
a. A frog
b. A school
c. A ghost
d. An eclipse

5. If you give an overview of a movie, you ________.
a. describe the important parts
b. watch it again
c. tell others it was a good movie
d. pay money

Exercise 2

Fill in the blanks with the correct words from the word bank.

Word Bank

loaf	oracles	inward	behalf	orbit
rite	globe	provided	overview	relevant

I'm going on a trip halfway across the 1______________.
While I'm gone, Sarah will turn in my homework on my 2______________.

On our vacation to Africa, we got to witness an old Egyptian 3______________.
We weren't told all the details of it, but we were given a brief 4______________.

He 5______________ slices of bread for the children's sandwiches.
He can make several by baking a single 6______________ of bread.

Sometimes, I choose to keep my thoughts and feelings 7______________.
Though I'm quiet about them, they are still 8______________ .

In the past, people asked 9______________ how the gods moved the planets.
Today, science explains how the planets 10______________ the sun.

Exercise 3

Choose the one that is similar in meaning to the given word.

1. relevant
   a. important b. beautiful c. vast d. different
2. horizontal
   a. heavy b. flat c. large d. nice
3. a rite
   a. a story b. a belief c. a body d. a ceremony
4. stall
   a. to stop b. to fade c. to blink d. to react
5. inventory
   a. a brand b. a trait c. a supply d. a car

Exercise 4

Write a word that is similar in meaning to the underlined part.

1. My earlier report was just a short account of the long, difficult book.

   ____

2. In ancient Greece, the person who gives advice often gave information about the future.

   ____

3. The top of the fence was perfectly flat and level with the ground.

   ____

4. I know about the piece because I saw the viewing before it was available to the public.

   ____

5. The baker made an extra piece of bread for the homeless man in the alley.

   ____

6. She is embarrassed of some of her not expressed or shown thoughts.

   ____

7. The fisherman liked to make a low, continuous noise while he waited for a bite.

   ____

8. The travelers were given a place to stay, but they had to supply their own food.

   ____

9. The company had to stop the process of the production of the dangerous toy.

   ____

10. We saw a cute polar bear jump into the water from the edge of the large mass of ice.

    ____

Cosmo's Flight

When Cosmo woke up, he was crying. He had a dream that he was falling. This dream had **recurred** for the **previous** five nights. Cosmo was scared that his dreams were a **preview** of what was going to happen on his flight the next day.

Cosmo was a **supernatural** being who was about to turn 15 years old. In his culture, boys of his age were required to participate in an important **rite**. They were given wings and instructed to **orbit** the Earth. After successful flights, the boys officially became men. Cosmo certainly wanted to be a man, but he was scared. He went to the **oracle** of a god named Dano. Cosmo said, "I'm not sure I can make such a long trip. What if I get tired? What if my strength **stalls,** and I can't stay in the air. I'll crash and die!"

Dano replied, "Don't be afraid. You have all the **relevant** skills in your personal **inventory** that have been building up over the years. To ease your worry, let me tell you a little about what will happen tomorrow. You'll begin over Africa. You'll keep flying north until you come to the Himalayas. The mountaintops will look like small **loaves** of bread at such a high distance. The rivers of the world will look like pieces of blue string that cross the **globe**. Keep your body **horizontal** when flying against the winds of the Pacific Ocean. Keep your eyes open and enjoy the beauty of the Earth. You will be fine, you'll see."

Cosmo replied, "Thanks for the **overview** of my journey, I'll do my best."

The next morning, Cosmo was **provided** with a divine set of wings and sent on his way. He **flapped** his wings and went high above the Earth. He flew over mountains, oceans, and **glaciers**. After a while, his **inward** thoughts were no longer about falling. He was actually having fun! He began to **hum** a song as he enjoyed the view. When he reached home, his tribe was there to greet him.

The chief said, "On **behalf** of the tribe, I declare you a man. We're proud of you, Cosmo!"

Cosmo was proud of himself, too.

Reading Comprehension

PART A Mark each statement T for true or F for false. Rewrite the false statements to make them true.

1. ____ Cosmo was scared that his recurring dreams of the previous nights were a preview of what would happen.

   ____

2. ____ Supernatural boys of Cosmo's age participated in an important rite.

   ____

3. ____ In Dano's summary, he told Cosmo to keep his body horizontal against the winds of the Indian Ocean.

   ____

4. ____ Dano flapped the wings he was provided with and orbited the globe.

   ____

5. ____ Cosmo sang a tune while he flew and enjoyed the view.

   ____

PART B Answer the questions.

1. What inward thoughts were no longer relevant to Cosmo after he started having fun?

   ____

   ____

2. What did Dano tell Cosmo that the tops of the Himalaya Mountains will look like?

   ____

   ____

3. What did Cosmo say after he thanked the oracle for the overview?

   ____

   ____

4. The oracle told Cosmo that the rivers of the world will look like what?

   ____

   ____

5. What did the chief declare on behalf of the tribe?

   ____

   ____

UNIT 27

Word List

adapt [ədǽpt] *v.*

To **adapt** means to change in order to deal with a new situation or addition.
→ *When he went to the new town, he had to **adapt** to all the weather changes.*

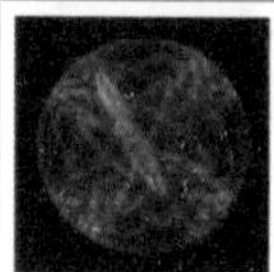

biological [bàiəlɑ́dʒikəl] *adj.*

Biological describes the process of life and living things.
→ *In science, we learned about the **biological** process of bacterial growth.*

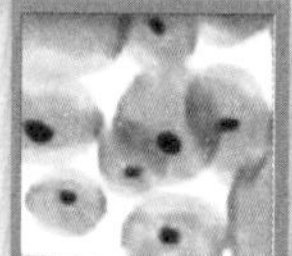

cellular [séljələr] *adj.*

When something is **cellular,** it relates to the cells of animals or plants.
→ *She used a microscope to see the activity at a **cellular** level.*

dynamic [dainǽmik] *adj.*

When people are **dynamic,** they are lively and have creative ideas.
→ *The new, **dynamic** employee came up with a good way to juggle his work load.*

fantasy [fǽntəsi] *n.*

A **fantasy** is a pleasant situation that people think about but is unlikely to happen.
→ *Becoming an astronaut is a **fantasy** shared by many children.*

heredity [hirédəti] *n.*

Heredity is the process of passing on features from parents to children.
→ *The boy's face is similar to his father's because of **heredity.***

internal [intə́ːrnl] *adj.*

When something is **internal,** it exists or happens inside a person, object, or place.
→ *We removed the outer case to reveal the computer's **internal** wires.*

minimal [minəməl] *adj.*

When something is **minimal,** it is very small.
→ *My lazy husband does a **minimal** amount of work around the house.*

pioneer [pàiəníər] *n.*

A **pioneer** is a person who is the first to discover or be involved in something.
→ *He was a **pioneer** of computer programming.*

prescribe [priskráib] *v.*

To **prescribe** medicine means to tell someone to take it.
→ *When I was sick, the doctor **prescribed** me flu medicine.*

respective [rispéktiv] *adj.*

When things are **respective**, they relate separately to each person just mentioned.

→ *The boxers were told to return to their **respective** corners.*

revive [riváiv] *v.*

To **revive** someone or something means to restore health or life to them.

→ *She **revived** the feeling of warmth in her leg by rubbing it softly.*

rigid [rídʒid] *adj.*

When rules or systems are **rigid**, they are severe because they cannot be changed.

→ *Societies often have **rigid** rules about the way that people are supposed to act.*

sequence [síːkwəns] *n.*

A **sequence** is a number of events or things that come one after another.

→ *The dominos fell in a **sequence** of one after another.*

substitute [sʌ́bstitjùːt] *v.*

To **substitute** something or someone means to have them take the place of another.

→ *When I ran out of juice, I had to **substitute** water to drink in the morning.*

surgeon [sə́ːrdʒən] *n.*

A **surgeon** is a doctor who is trained to do surgery.

→ *The **surgeon** operated on the old man's heart.*

therapy [θérəpi] *n.*

Therapy is treatment for a particular physical or mental illness or condition.

→ *After she broke her legs, she used physical **therapy** to learn how to walk again.*

transfer [trænsfə́ːr] *v.*

To **transfer** something means to move it from one place to another.

→ *The family **transferred** the groceries from the shopping cart to the car.*

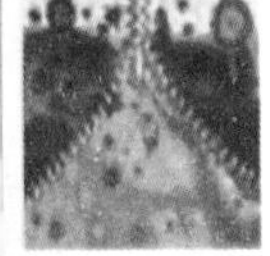

transition [trænzíʃən] *n.*

A **transition** is a process where there is a change from one form to another.

→ *The weather gets colder during the **transition** from summer to autumn.*

transplant [trǽnsplæ̀nt] *n.*

A **transplant** is an operation in which a damaged part of one's body is replaced.

→ *The sick child needed a heart **transplant** to live.*

Exercise 1

Choose the answer that best fits the question.

1. What thing is a result of heredity?
   a. Eye color b. Clothing style c. A haircut d. A job
2. What process is biological?
   a. Walking to school b. Taking a test c. Producing tears d. Getting dressed
3. What is something that is prescribed?
   a. A car b. A report card c. A cold medicine d. An illness
4. What might be transplanted?
   a. A file b. A liver c. A can d. A shoe
5. What does a surgeon wear?
   a. Gloves b. Thick boots c. A swimming suit d. Goggles

Exercise 2

Write a word that is similar in meaning to the underlined part.

1. The child received treatment for his mental condition after he became depressed.

   ____

2. The medical students learned which processes were occurring inside living things.

   ____

3. Unicorns only exist in a situation people think about but will not happen.

   ____

4. When he begins his rule, people will have to change to the new situation.

   ____

5. At the relating to cells level, plants and animals are quite similar.

   ____

6. We thought his rules were too severe because they cannot be changed.

   ____

7. The lively and creative scientist invented a new formula to help stop aging.

   ____

8. The creative inventor was a first person to discover the process of electricity.

   ____

9. There is a specific number of events that come in an order in which to use the tools.

   ____

10. The brilliant doctor brought back to life the dead patient.

    ____

Exercise 3

Write C if the italicized word is used correctly. Write I if the word is used incorrectly.

1. ____ The *surgeon* made a small cut into the patient's skin.

2. ____ The building materials must be *transferred* to the new site.

3. ____ The *rigid* rules were confusing because they changed all the time.

4. ____ The baby *prescribed* his mother to get a piece of candy.

5. ____ You can observe water's *transition* into ice when the temperature gets cold.

6. ____ Blood flow is a *biological* process.

7. ____ I never want to get a new house, so I *substitute* the one I have.

8. ____ The *dynamic* teacher thought of new and exciting teaching methods.

9. ____ Going to sleep at night is a *fantasy*.

10. ____ He needed plenty of rest after his liver *transplant*.

11. ____ The pieces must be put on the machine in the correct *sequence*.

12. ____ I admired how often he chose to be *respective*.

13. ____ My ney school is great. I can't *adapt* to my classes.

14. ____ Hot dogs are one of my favorite surgical foods to *revive*.

15. ____ The *heredity* expert can tell us how traits are passed on from a father.

16. ____ Please take the big, *cellular* pieces to the recycling center.

17. ____ The hours of *therapy* were worth it when I could move my arm again.

18. ____ He's always the last to understand a joke. He's such a *pioneer*.

19. ____ The *internal* roof got covered in snow after the storm.

20. ____ I was still hungry because I only ate a *minimal* amount of food at dinner.

The First Organ Transplant

In 1954, a man named Richard was dying of kidney disease. He wouldn't survive for long unless he got a new kidney right away. Richard's twin brother, Robert, was willing to donate one of his kidneys to his dying brother. At the time, however, no doctor had ever performed a successful **internal** organ **transplant**. The idea of taking an organ out of one person and putting it into another was just a **fantasy**. But the brothers decided to be brave and found a doctor who could make organ transplants a reality.

Since Richard and Robert were twins, their **heredity** was identical. They had the exact same **biological** traits. Even their kidneys were identical on the **cellular** level. Therefore, Robert's working kidney could be **substituted** for Richard's bad one. Richard's body could **adapt** to the new organ if the operation was done correctly.

The twins went to Dr. Murray, who was a **pioneer** of new surgical methods. His **dynamic** team of **surgeons** performed the transplant. Dr. Murray made sure his surgeons followed a **rigid sequence** of directions so that no mistakes were made. First, they made a **minimal** cut in Richard's side and removed the bad kidney. Then, they made another small cut in Robert's side, removed his kidney, and **transferred** it into Richard's body. Finally, they sewed up the **respective** cuts. The entire operation only took about one hour.

After the surgery, it was clear that both brothers were going to be OK. The operation was confirmed a success. Richard's new kidney worked great! Doctors **prescribed** medicine for the pain caused by the surgery. Since Richard was still weak, he used physical **therapy** to **revive** his strength. At last, Richard's **transition** into a healthy, happy person was complete.

Dr. Murray became a hero in the medical world. His success gave other doctors confidence to try organ transplants themselves. Now, doctors perform life-saving transplants and surgeries every day.

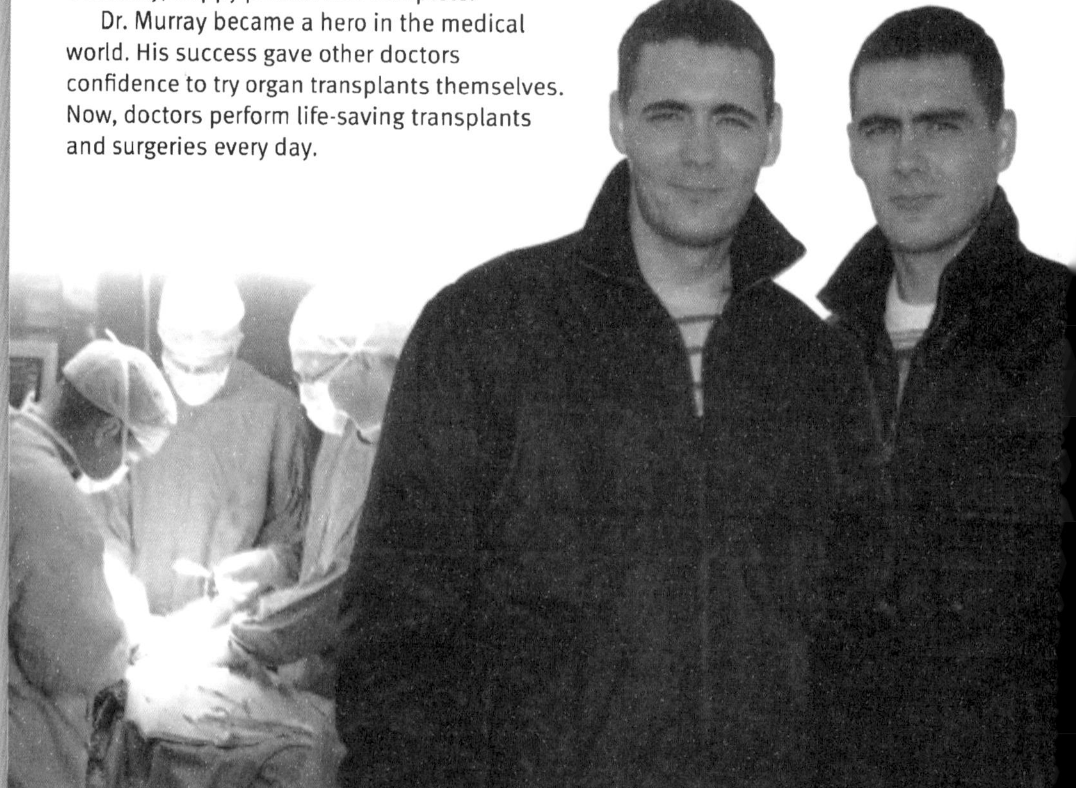

Reading Comprehension

PART A Mark each statement T for true or F for false. Rewrite the false statements to make them true.

1. ____ Internal organ transplants were a fantasy after 1954.

2. ____ Robert was a pioneer of new surgical procedures.

3. ____ The twins' kidneys were identical on the cellular level because of their heredity.

4. ____ The dynamic surgeons followed a rigid sequence of directions to avoid mistakes.

5. ____ Richard's body adapted to the kidney that was transferred from his brother.

PART B Answer the questions.

1. What was substituted in the passage?

2. What was true of the twin's biological traits?

3. What did the doctors prescribe to revive Richard's strength?

4. Where did the surgeons make minimal cuts in the respective bodies of each twin?

5. What was the result of Richard's transition after his therapy?

UNIT 28

Word List

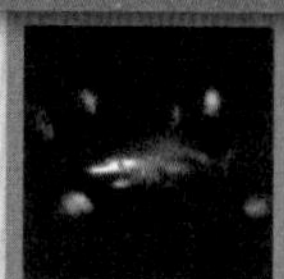

aquarium [əkwɛ́əriəm] *n.*

An **aquarium** is a building where fish and underwater animals are kept.
→ *We took a trip to the* ***aquarium*** *and saw a scary shark.*

arbitrary [ɑ́:rbitreri] *adj.*

If something is **arbitrary,** it is not based on any plan or system, so it seems random.
→ *The classroom had many* ***arbitrary*** *rules that made me confused.*

autobiography [ɔ̀:təbaiɑ́grəfi] *n.*

An **autobiography** is a true story of a person's life written by that person.
→ *I read an* ***autobiography*** *about my favorite entertainer.*

convention [kənvénʃən] *n.*

A **convention** is behavior that is considered to be common or polite.
→ *In the US, a popular* ***convention*** *is to shake hands when you meet someone.*

gracious [gréiʃəs] *adj.*

If someone is **gracious,** then they are kind and helpful to those who need it.
→ *The operator was* ***gracious*** *enough to help me find his number.*

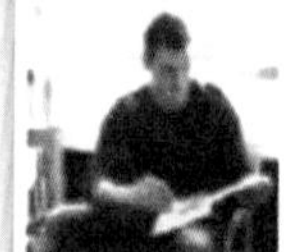

improve [imprú:v] *v.*

To **improve** something means to make it better.
→ *He studied hard to* ***improve*** *his test scores from the previous year.*

insulate [insəlèit] *v.*

To **insulate** something means to protect it from heat, cold, or noise.
→ *People can conserve energy by* ***insulating*** *their houses.*

intrigue [intri g] *v.*

To **intrigue** means to cause an interest in something or someone.
→ *Her mysterious past* ***intrigued*** *her new friend.*

longevity [lɑndʒévəti] *n.*

Longevity is the ability to live for a long time.
→ *Sea turtles have an amazing* ***longevity.***

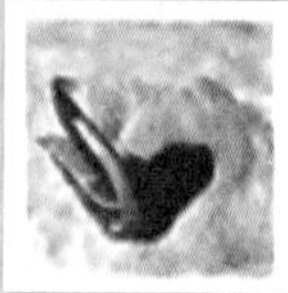

misplace [mispléis] *v.*

To **misplace** something means to lose it.
→ ***I misplaced*** *my wallet, and I didn't find it until a week later.*

naughty [nɔ́:ti] *adj.*

When children are **naughty,** they behave badly or do not do what they are told.

→ *The boy had to go to his room because he was being **naughty**.*

norm [nɔ:rm] *n.*

A **norm** is a way of behaving that is considered normal in a particular society.

→ *Wearing a heavy coat all summer is not considered a **norm** in the desert.*

orangutan [ɔ:rǽŋutæ̀n] *n.*

An **orangutan** is a large ape with red and brown hair and long arms.

→ ***Orangutans** use their long arms to swing from trees.*

overload [òuvərlóud] *v.*

To **overload** something means to put more things into it than it is meant to hold.

→ *If you **overload** the truck, it might crash.*

philanthropy [filǽnθrəpi] *n.*

Philanthropy is the act of helping others, without wanting anything in return.

→ *The wealthy business owner is well known for his acts of **philanthropy**.*

probe [proub] *v.*

To **probe** into something means to ask questions to discover facts about it.

→ *The bank **probed** into his financial history to see if he qualified for a loan.*

recipient [risípiənt] *n.*

A **recipient** of something is the person who receives it.

→ *I was the **recipient** of four phone calls today.*

reptile [réptail] *n.*

A **reptile** is a cold-blooded animal that lays eggs and has skin covered with scales.

→ *Lizards are my favorite type of **reptile**.*

thrive [θraiv] *v.*

To **thrive** means to do well and be successful, healthy, or strong.

→ *He may be an old man, but he continues to **thrive**.*

ultimate [ʌ́ltəmit] *adj.*

When something is **ultimate,** it is the final result or aim of a long series of events.

→ *By trying hard in school, I will reach my **ultimate** goal of becoming a doctor.*

Exercise 1

Choose the answer that best fits the question.

1. What would you find at an aquarium?
   a. A blanket
   b. A squid
   c. A cow
   d. A coyote
2. What can you do to improve your grades?
   a. Copy them
   b. Study more
   c. Miss class
   d. Get less sleep
3. What is the ultimate result of going to college?
   a. Signing up for classes
   b. Taking many tests
   c. Getting a degree
   d. Dating
4. What happens if you insulate a house in the winter?
   a. Cold air stays outside.
   b. Fires cannot be lit.
   c. You can never get outside.
   d. It will float.
5. Who would most likely publish an autobiography?
   a. An important person
   b. A five-year-old
   c. A shy teenager
   d. A dead person

Exercise 2

Choose the one that is opposite in meaning to the given word.

1. recipient
   a. an attempt b. a giver c. a friend d. a follower
2. misplace
   a. to try b. to help c. to find d. to declare
3. naughty
   a. wanting more b. over c. lacking d. behaving well
4. longevity
   a. short life b. plans c. answers d. tallness
5. thrive
   a. to create b. to do bad c. to agree d. to move around
6. gracious
   a. mean b. silly c. kind d. smart
7. norm
   a. abnormal b. common c. everyday d. average
8. intrigue
   a. to excite b. to bore c. to reassure d. to trust
9. arbitrary
   a. accidental b. solar c. random d. planned
10. probe
    a. to touch b. to open c. to ignore d. to build

Exercise 3

Write C if the italicized word is used correctly. Write I if the word is used incorrectly.

1. ____ Make sure to *misplace* your money so that you will always have it.
2. ____ The *orangutans* at the zoo swung so gracefully from the trees.
3. ____ The tigers in the *aquarium* loved to run and play.
4. ____ The greedy man loved *philanthropy*. He never offered to help anybody.
5. ____ The box broke when he *overloaded* it with books.
6. ____ The mechanics of computers *intrigue* me.
7. ____ The *longevity* of the rat was fifty centimeters.
8. ____ Plants will *thrive* if they are not given any water.
9. ____ The *naughty* girl always obeyed her mother.
10. ____ The *ultimate* result of the game was a win for the home team.
11. ____ Some people play the lottery in hopes that they will *improve* their lives.
12. ____ Paying for gasoline before pumping it is a *norm*.
13. ____ I *probed* the audience because I didn't want to hear what they had to say.
14. ____ Waiting your turn in line is a social *convention*.
15. ____ My dog is a great *reptile*.
16. ____ I *insulated* my room with blankets to keep the loud noises out.
17. ____ She was the *recipient* of the grand prize.
18. ____ Someday, I will write my father's *autobiography*.
19. ____ I don't want to play with you anymore. You make up *arbitrary* rules as we play.
20. ____ The store clerk was so *gracious*. He helped me find everything I was looking for.

The Lottery

Joe was watching television when he heard a knock at the door. He thought, "Who could that be? It's probably one of the **naughty** neighborhood children." Joe stood up and walked to the door. When he opened it, he saw a beautiful woman.

She said, "Good morning, Joe! I have great news. You're the **recipient** of this check for one million dollars! You won the lottery!"

Joe couldn't believe it. His mind was **overloaded** with emotions. Joe said, "Thank you! Thank you!"

After he calmed down, Joe made a photocopy of the check in case he **misplaced** the original one. He sat and thought about what he wanted to do with the money. He didn't want to spend it in an **arbitrary** way. Joe thought, "I know there are others who need this money more than I do. I've always loved animals, so I think I'll buy things for the zoo!"

Joe knew that the zoo was in bad shape. The cages were too small, and they weren't **insulated** from the cold. Animals couldn't **thrive** in such conditions.

He took out some stationery and wrote a letter to the zoo. He offered to help the zoo buy huge cages for the large mammals and **reptiles.** He offered to buy healthy food for the **orangutans** to increase their **longevity**. He even said that he would buy new glass walls for the **aquarium** because the old ones were cracked.

Joe's act of **philanthropy intrigued** the zookeeper. He **probed** Joe to learn why he spent his money to **improve** the zoo. It wasn't a social **convention** for a person to be so **gracious**.

Joe told the zookeeper, "I know it's not the **norm**, but my **ultimate** decision to help these animals is better than anything I could have done for myself. If I ever write an **autobiography**, I will write that this was the happiest day of my life."

Reading Comprehension

PART A Mark each statement T for true or F for false. Rewrite the false statements to make them true.

1. ____ Joe was the recipient of a check because he won the lottery.

____

2. ____ He wanted to buy new glass walls for the aquarium because the old ones were cracked.

____

3. ____ If Joe wrote an autobiography, he would write about the norms of the overloaded aquarium.

____

4. ____ Joe made a photocopy of the check in case he misplaced the original one.

____

5. ____ When Joe opened the door, he saw one of the naughty neighborhood children.

____

PART B Answer the questions.

1. What did Joe think the naughty children were doing to him?

____

____

2. Why did Joe take out stationery?

____

____

3. What did Joe improve to help the orangutans increase their longevity?

____

____

4. What was the purpose of the zookeeper wanting to probe Joe with questions?

____

____

5. If Joe were to write an autobiography, how would he describe this day?

____

____

UNIT 29

Word List

antique [æntíːk] *adj.*

If something is **antique**, it is very old and rare, and therefore valuable.
→ *My grandmother's **antique** rocking chair is worth a lot of money.*

applicant [ǽplikənt] *n.*

An **applicant** is someone who writes a request to be considered for a job or prize.
→ *Lots of **applicants** came into the store when the job position became available.*

artifact [ɑ́ːrtəfæ̀kt] *n.*

An **artifact** is an old object made by humans that is historically interesting.
→ *We studied **artifacts** from an ancient Chinese settlement.*

authentic [ɔːθéntik] *adj.*

When something is **authentic**, it is not false or a copy of the original.
→ *We ate **authentic** Italian food on our vacation to Rome.*

chronology [krənɑ́lədʒi] *n.*

The **chronology** of a series of past events is when they happened.
→ *We learned the **chronology** of World War II in history class.*

diplomat [dípləmæ̀t] *n.*

A **diplomat** is a representative of a country who works with another country.
→ *The Spanish **diplomat** discussed trade issues with officials in Peru.*

epic [épik] *n.*

An **epic** is a long book, poem, or movie about a period of time or a great event.
→ *The poet wrote an **epic** about the great discoveries of the past thousand years.*

excerpt [eksəːrpt] *n.*

An **excerpt** is a short piece of writing or music taken from a larger piece.
→ *I didn't listen to the entire symphony online, but I did play an **excerpt**.*

fossil [fɑ́sl] *n.*

A **fossil** is the hard remains of a prehistoric animal or plant.
→ *The expert arranged the **fossils** to build the skeleton of the dinosaur.*

humiliate [hjuːmílieit] *v.*

To **humiliate** someone means to make them feel ashamed and embarrassed.
→ *I was **humiliated** when I tripped and fell down in front of the whole school.*

lyric [lírik] *adj.*
When a poem is considered **lyric**, it is written in a simple and direct style.
→ *I enjoy reading and creating my own **lyric** poetry.*

majesty [mǽdʒisti] *n.*
Majesty is supreme greatness or authority.
→ *You should address the king and queen as your **majesty**.*

monarch [mɑ́nərk] *n.*
The **monarch** of a country is the king, queen, emperor, or empress.
→ *The **monarch** lived in a beautiful palace with a grand gate.*

precede [prisí:d] *v.*
To **precede** something means to come before it.
→ *The hurricane was **preceded** by a moment of still wind and clear sky.*

punctual [pʌ́ŋktʃuəl] *adj.*
When someone is **punctual**, they do something or arrive at the right time.
→ *My mother hates being late. She is the most **punctual** person I know.*

recruit [rikrú:t] *v.*
To **recruit** people means to select them to join or work for an organization.
→ *We successfully **recruited** someone to be the new manager.*

refund [ri:fʌnd] *n.*
A **refund** is money given back to a person when an item is returned to a store.
→ *I asked for a **refund** because the shoes I bought were too tight.*

register [rédʒəstə:r] *n.*
A **register** is an official list or record of people or things.
→ *At a wedding there is **register** for all of the guests to sign.*

renown [rináun] *n.*
Renown is the quality of being well known due to having done good things.
→ *Michael is a singer of great **renown** in New Zealand.*

tusk [tʌsk] *n.*
A **tusk** is a long, curved, pointed tooth of an elephant, boar, or walrus.
→ *Sadly, some people hunt elephants and remove their **tusks** to sell them.*

Exercise 1

Choose the answer that best fits the question.

1. Which of the following might humiliate someone?
a. Spilling a drink
b. Getting a new car
c. Working ten hours
d. Sitting down

2. What might be antique?
a. A sweet fruit
b. An old sofa
c. A good father
d. A cell phone

3. Who is referred to as her majesty?
a. A queen
b. A student
c. A mother
d. A teacher

4. Where might a job applicant go for job?
a. An abandoned house
b. A store with an available position
c. A sandy beach
d. A graveyard

5. What precedes waking up in the morning?
a. Going to sleep
b. Going to school
c. Buying a new bed
d. Shopping

Exercise 2

Fill in the blanks with the correct words from the word bank.

Word Bank

antique	refund	monarch	artifact	authentic
register	Majesty	tusks	fossil	applicants

The statue of the walrus had long, beautiful **1**______________.
The **2**______________ piece was over a hundred years old and quite valuable.

Many stories have been told about the powerful **3**______________.
All of the king's servants addressed him as "Your **4**______________."

The college must decide who to accept among thousands of **5**______________.
The most qualified will add their names to the elite **6**______________.

I now see that my new leather boots are not **7**______________.
I need to take these fake boots back to the store and get a **8**______________.

Mark thought that the old bone he found was a dinosaur **9**______________.
However, it turned out to be a man-made **10**______________.

Exercise 3

Choose the one that is similar in meaning to the given word.

1. humiliate
   a. impress b. entertain c. destroy d. embarrass
2. diplomat
   a. a representative b. a user c. a creature d. a joker
3. punctual
   a. hurried b. on time c. too loud d. brave
4. precede
   a. to fail b. to quit c. to rely d. to go first
5. register
   a. a control b. a list c. an apartment d. a grave

Exercise 4

Write a word that is similar in meaning to the underlined part.

1. The circus performer held on to the elephant's <u>long, curved tooth</u>.

   ____

2. The salesman assured me that the artwork was <u>not false or an imitation</u>.

   ____

3. At the end of the year, our club will <u>select</u> a new person to join.

   ____

4. Janet isn't <u>able to arrive at the right time</u> at all. She's late to school every day.

   ____

5. It is difficult to follow the <u>series of past events and times</u> of computer programming.

   ____

6. DNA can be taken from a <u>part of hard remains from a prehistoric animal</u>.

   ____

7. Please stand and read a(an) <u>short piece of writing taken from a larger piece</u>.

   ____

8. I took a class at the university where I wrote <u>simple and direct</u> poetry.

   ____

9. *The Iliad* is an wonderful <u>long book about great events</u>.

   ____

10. Her mother was a dancer of some <u>quality of being well known for doing good things</u>.

    ____

Jen's New Job

The history museum needed to **recruit** a new tour guide. The director interviewed dozens of **applicants** before he decided to hire Jen. She was chosen because she was friendly, **punctual** and had a great attitude.

On her first day, Jen got to work and prepared to give her first tour. She looked at the names on the **register**. She saw that the Queen of England and a **diplomat** were visiting the museum. She thought, "It's my very first day, and I have to impress a **monarch**! I hope I don't **humiliate** myself in front of a person of such **renown**!"

Jen was nervous. She took a deep breath and said, "Hello, everyone! I'm going to talk to you about the **chronology** of ancient Egypt." As she turned around to show the group some **artifacts**, she bumped into a **fossil** of an **authentic** elephant **tusk**. It fell to the ground and broke into a million pieces! "Oh no!" said Jen in a subtle voice. "I sure hope the rest of the tour goes better than this!"

The rest of the tour did not go any better. She tripped over an **antique** vase and broke a piece off of it. As she was reading an **excerpt** from a **lyric** poem, she sneezed and tore a page of the **epic**.

After the tour, Jen approached the queen to apologize. She said, "I'm sorry, Your **Majesty**. I was a terrible tour guide. Let me give you a **refund** for the money you spent."

The queen laughed. She said, "I don't want my money back, Jen. I loved the tour. You just have to be a little more careful and work hard to become the best at your job. Hard work **precedes** success."

Jen smiled and thanked the queen. She decided to be extra careful from then on. She was persistent and worked hard. In time, Jen became the best tour guide at the museum.

Reading Comprehension

PART A Mark each statement T for true or F for false. Rewrite the false statements to make them true.

1. ____ The museum director interviewed dozens of applicants when he recruited a new tour guide.

____

2. ____ Jen did not want to humiliate herself in front of the diplomat and the monarch.

____

3. ____ The queen bumped into the fossil of an authentic elephant tusk.

____

4. ____ Jen was chosen for the job because she was friendly, punctual, and had a register.

____

5. ____ Jen broke artifacts, including an antique vase.

____

PART B Answer the questions.

1. What did Jen say she hoped for in a subtle voice?

____

____

2. What chronology did Jen want to talk about to her tour group?

____

____

3. What happened as Jen was reading the excerpt from the epic lyric poem?

____

____

4. Why did Jen offer her majesty a refund?

____

____

5. What precedes success, according to the queen?

____

____

Word List

burden [bə́:rdn] *n.*

A **burden** is a serious or difficult responsibility.

→ *Children who do not behave are a* ***burden*** *to their parents.*

compromise [kámprəmàiz] *v.*

To **compromise** is to agree to something that is not exactly what you want.

→ *We both* ***compromised*** *about the game we decided to play.*

craft [kræft] *v.*

To **craft** something is to make it using skill.

→ *She* ***crafted*** *the bookcase out of solid pine wood and then painted it.*

crook [kruk] *n.*

A **crook** is someone who is not honest or who commits crimes.

→ *The manager was arrested by the police for being a* ***crook.***

currency [kə́:rənsi] *n.*

Currency is the form of money used in a certain place.

→ *Elizabeth had to exchange her dollars for foreign* ***currency.***

enigma [inigmə] *n.*

An **enigma** is someone or something that is mysterious or hard to understand.

→ *The theft of the paintings is an* ***enigma*** *to the investigators.*

fragile [frǽdʒəl] *adj.*

When people or things are **fragile,** they are not strong and can be damaged easily.

→ *The* ***fragile*** *glassware was carefully packed into boxes.*

hybrid [háibrid] *n.*

A **hybrid** is a mixture of different things or styles.

→ *In Greek mythology, a centaur is a* ***hybrid*** *of a man and a horse.*

innocence [inəsns] *n.*

Innocence is a lack of experience of difficult or complex things in life.

→ *Everyone who met her found her* ***innocence*** *to be charming.*

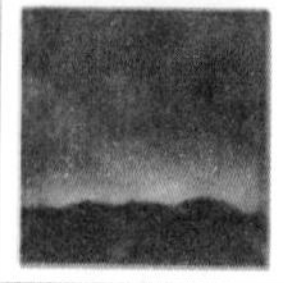

merge [mə:rdʒ] *v.*

To **merge** two things is to combine them into one whole thing.

→ *The storm clouds* ***merged*** *into one large menacing cloud that filled the sky.*

moderate [mɑ́dərèit] *adj.*

When something is **moderate**, it is not too big or too small in size or amount.

→ *It takes a **moderate** amount of patience to be around small children all day.*

overwhelm [òuvərhwélm] *v.*

To **overwhelm** is to exist in such a large amount that someone cannot deal with it.

→ *The amount of homework her teacher assigned has **overwhelmed** her.*

perception [pərsépʃən] *n.*

A **perception** of a situation is a way of thinking about it or understanding it.

→ *Since he couldn't see, his **perception** of life was much different than mine.*

reunion [ri:jú:njən] *n.*

A **reunion** is the meeting of people or things that have been separated.

→ *Every summer we have a family **reunion** at the lake.*

rig [rig] *v.*

To **rig** something means to dishonestly arrange it.

→ *The bad politician **rigged** the election so that he would win.*

shiver [ʃívə:r] *n.*

A **shiver** is a shaking movement the body makes when someone is cold or scared.

→ *I got **shivers** on my way home because it was so cold.*

sociable [sóuʃəbəl] *adj.*

When someone is **sociable**, they are friendly.

→ *Many of my good friends are **sociable**, but I am shy.*

talkative [tɔ́:kətiv] *adj.*

When someone is **talkative**, they talk a lot.

→ *My aunt is very **talkative** whenever she is on the phone.*

tow [tou] *v.*

To **tow** something is to pull it.

→ *The truck was **towing** a trailer behind it.*

tramp [træmp] *v.*

To **tramp** is to put your feet down in a loud, heavy way as you walk.

→ *The baby **tramped** across the floor as he was learning to walk.*

Exercise 1

Choose the answer that best fits the question.

1. If you are an enigma, you are _______.
   a. funny b. mysterious c. dishonest d. sleepy
2. If someone is too talkative during a movie, then others may _______.
   a. get sleepy b. get angry c. start to sing d. join in
3. If someone has shivers, what should they do?
   a. Stop running b. Put on a sweater c. Be quiet d. Sit down
4. How should someone deal with another that is overwhelming them?
   a. Ask for help b. Forget it c. Keep quite d. Cry
5. Which of the following would have the most innocence?
   a. A grandparent b. A sea captain c. A teen d. A president
6. What would someone consider a burden?
   a. Working two jobs b. A happy child c. Resting d. Taking a walk
7. If someone exercised a moderate amount, they would be _______.
   a. stressed b. healthy c. very ill d. a good leader
8. Who would you probably see at a reunion?
   a. Your family b. The police c. Your boss d. Your barber
9. Where would a crook most likely end up for doing something wrong?
   a. At church b. In jail c. In school d. On vacation
10. What is a boat most likely to tow behind it?
    a. A trailer b. A water skier c. A fisherman d. A rocket

Exercise 2

Write a word that is similar in meaning to the underlined part.

1. I met a very <u>friendly</u> girl on my first day of school.

   ____

2. Marty <u>walked heavily</u> across the kitchen to the back door.

   ____

3. That lovely dresser was <u>skillfully made</u> from oak.

   ____

4. The man had <u>dishonestly changed</u> the game so that he would win every time.

   ____

5. The paint colors <u>combined</u> to make new ones on the canvas.

   ____

Exercise 3

Choose the one that is similar in meaning to the given word.

1. fragile
a. sturdy b. strong c. robust d. weak

2. shiver
a. jump b. fall c. shake d. stand

3. currency
a. money b. recent c. waves d. spend

4. overwhelm
a. too much b. not enough c. completed d. unfinished

5. sociable
a. rude b. friendly c. cunning d. wise

6. craft
a. to bend b. to make c. to ruin d. to stir

7. enigma
a. public b. dramatic c. mystery d. parent

8. crook
a. thief b. hermit c. wizard d. warrior

9. merge
a. to pull apart b. to float c. to carry d. to combine

10. burden
a. a deal b. a resolution c. an order d. a hard responsibility

Exercise 4

Write C if the italicized word is used correctly. Write I if the word is used incorrectly.

1. ____ Let's *compromise* and do exactly what I want.

2. ____ Jill's *perception* of the movie was opposite to many viewers.

3. ____ The temperature in here is too *moderate*. I'm freezing!

4. ____ We had a *reunion* yesterday. I haven't seen her for years.

5. ____ Tonya's new car is a *hybrid* that runs on gas and electricity.

6. ____ It is such *burden* to drive two hours to work each day.

7. ____ The *enigma* was so simple that a child could find a solution.

8. ____ Her *innocence* reminded many of us when we were young.

9. ____ I *crafted* the airplane out of pieces of old wood.

10. ____ The snake *tramped* quietly on its stomach.

The Demon's Bridge

A young woman's cow had crossed the river in the morning when the water level was **moderate**. But when the woman returned with her dog to get the cow, she was **overwhelmed** by how high the water had risen. Even if she crossed, she still couldn't **tow** her cow back through the river.

"What am I going to do?" she wondered.

Suddenly, a man appeared across the river. "A **fragile** young lady like you shouldn't have to struggle across a river," he said. "I'll build you a bridge."

The man was an **enigma**. The young woman's **perception** of him was that he was a **sociable** person. He was **talkative**, yet something was strange about him.

"I don't want to be a **burden** to you, sir," the woman replied.

"Don't worry," he told her as he began **crafting** a bridge. He **merged** the pieces of the bridge together with amazing speed. Soon, it was finished.

"Oh, but how can I pay you for your work? Let's **compromise**. I am sure that we can find a fair solution. What do you think?" The woman asked.

"The only **currency** I need is the first living thing that crosses the bridge," the man replied.

She thought, "This deal sounds weird. Maybe he's actually a river demon." She **shivered** because she realized that he had taken advantage of her **innocence** and **rigged** the deal somehow. But she had a plan of her own. She pulled a piece of bread from her pocket and threw it across the bridge. Her dog ran after it.

"The dog is the first living thing across the bridge," she said to the man.

The man was angry. He suddenly changed into a **hybrid** of a human and a fish. "You **crook**!" he shouted. "You tricked me. I have no use for your dog!" He screamed and dove into the river.

The woman **tramped** across the bridge to the other side and had a happy **reunion** with her dog and cow.

Reading Comprehension

PART A Mark each statement T for true or F for false. Rewrite the false statements to make them true.

1. ____ The woman's perception was that though the man was talkative and sociable, he was also an enigma.

____

2. ____ When the young woman returned, she was overwhelmed by the moderate water level.

____

3. ____ The fragile young woman thought she might be a burden to the man.

____

4. ____ While crafting the bridge, the man merged the pieces with amazing speed.

____

5. ____ The woman tramped across the bridge and had a happy reunion with the man.

____

PART B Answer the questions.

1. What did the man change into a hybrid of after the dog crossed the bridge?

____

____

2. Why was the young woman unable to tow her cow across the river?

____

____

3. What currency did the man ask to compromise?

____

____

4. Why did the young woman shiver?

____

____

5. What did the water demon call the woman just before he dove into the river?

____

____

Index

Index

Unit 1

Exercise 1
1. a
2. b
3. d
4. d
5. c
6. b
7. d
8. d
9. a
10. c

Exercise 2
1. b
2. a
3. c
4. a
5. d

Exercise 3
1. a
2. c
3. b
4. c
5. a

Exercise 4
1. C
2. C
3. I
4. C
5. I
6. I
7. I
8. C
9. C
10. I

Reading Comprehension
Part A
1. F …so she gathered a **massive** pile of beans for her cache.
2. T
3. T
4. T
5. F ... Mary had a **paltry** amount of food.

Part B
1. Beth's primary job was to gather food.
2. She thought that food would just come to her, and she wouldn't have to work.
3. Mary not having anything to eat.
4. Mary took the bag and went to work gathering beans.
5. She knew her sister was right.

Unit 2

Exercise 1
1. a
2. a
3. d
4. b
5. d

Exercise 2
1. prairie
2. rugged
3. arid
4. moisture
5. fast
6. cathedral
7. abundant
8. scarce
9. oath
10. eligible

Exercise 3
1. I
2. I
3. C
4. C
5. C

Exercise 4
1. arid
2. inland
3. drought
4. abbey
5. nonetheless
6. speculated
7. ample
8. adjoined
9. ragged
10. deprived

Reading Comprehension
Part A
1. T
2. T
3. F ...had to **help** the families nonetheless.
4. T
5. T

Part B
1. The abbot said, "All were eligible."
2. When the monks grumbled, the young monk speculated that if more families came, then they wouldn't make it through the winter.
3. The monks fasted and slept in the churchyard that adjoined the cathedral so that the families would have enough food and shelter.
4. The monks had taken an oath to help those that need help.
5. They learned that sometimes helping others means you must give more help than you first expected.

Unit 3

Exercise 1
1. b
2. d
3. c
4. a
5. d

Exercise 2
1. b
2. d
3. a
4. d
5. c
6. a
7. c
8. a
9. b
10. d

Exercise 3
1. I
2. I
3. C
4. C
5. C
6. I
7. C
8. I
9. I
10. C

Exercise 4
1. mythology
2. asserts
3. theoretical
4. radioactive
5. cognitive
6. celestial
7. diploma
8. relativity
9. keen
10. bachelors

Reading Comprehension
Part A
1. T
2. F ...the movements of **celestial objects** and how to harness the power of **radioactive substances** .
3. T
4. F ... geology **didn't give** the bachelor a wonderful feeling
5. F **Helping others**, not his cognitive talents, had ...

Part B
1. As soon as he had received his diploma, he asserted to everyone he met that he was the smartest person in town.
2. One day while strolling through the town, the bachelor witnessed a collision between two cars.
3. The bachelor felt the best he had in his entire life.
4. Despite his analytic abilities, he failed to notice he was missing something very important in his life.
5. Besides a brain, the bachelor realized that you must also have a heart.

Unit 4

Exercise 1
1. c
2. b
3. a
4. d
5. c
6. a
7. d
8. b
9. c
10. a

Exercise 2
1. I
2. C
3. I
4. I
5. C
6. C
7. I
8. I
9. C
10. C

Exercise 3
1. b
2. c
3. a
4. d
5. c

Exercise 4
1. incentive
2. transaction
3. legislated
4. bribed
5. retail
6. administrator
7. headquarters
8. corrupt
9. legitimate
10. revenue

Reading Comprehension

Part A
1. F Mr. **Pig** was an administrator...
2. F ...made to the factory were **not** legitimate.
3. T
4. F ...disposing of the factory's rubbish in the **river**.
5. F ...created **more** revenue.

Part B
1. His boss told him, "If the factory makes more money, then you will too."
2. After Pig automated his factory, the other animals had no jobs.
3. According to the officials, Pig manipulated the law in order to get more money.
4. When all transactions stopped, the factory lost money, and Pig lost his job.
5. The stores could no longer sell goods at retail because the machines didn't make products as well as the workers, and customers were disappointed with the factory's merchandise.

Unit 5

Exercise 1
1. d
2. a
3. d
4. b
5. c
6. a
7. c
8. b
9. d
10. d

Exercise 2
1. terminal
2. extract
3. impulse
4. subsequent
5. assess
6. ongoing
7. essence
8. fabulous
9. astonished
10. publicity

Exercise 3
1. haste
2. significance
3. molecules
4. commenced
5. proximity
6. latter
7. synthetic
8. assess
9. remedy
10. pharmaceutical

Reading Comprehension
Part A
1. T
2. T
3. F ...The infection caused by the bacteria he was working on was terminal.
4. T
5. F Whenever the **fungus was close to** the...

Part B
1. In his haste to go on vacation, Alexander Fleming left his laboratory in a mess.
2. The significance of the fungus was that it could kill the bacteria.
3. While he was cleaning, he had an impulse to examine the fungus.
4. The scientist extracted molecules from the fungus.
5. The discovery received a lot of publicity.

Unit 6

Exercise 1
1. d
2. a
3. b
4. c
5. d

Exercise 2
1. b
2. c
3. a
4. c
5. c
6. a
7. d
8. b
9. a
10. b

Exercise 3
1. I
2. C
3. C
4. I
5. C
6. C
7. I
8. I
9. C
10. C
11. C
12. I
13. I
14. C
15. C
16. I
17. I
18. C
19. C
20. C

Reading Comprehension
Part A
1. T
2. F Bob implemented a plan to **return home to his spouse and children.**
3. F **His shoulder injury** impaired his ability to carry the materials.
4. T
5. T

Part B
1. Insight about the island and finding something to help him escape.
2. Because he wanted to make it home.
3. He dragged tree limbs and vines.
4. By keeping a good attitude.
5. He believes that optimism and ambition make anything possible.

Unit 7

Exercise 1
1. temperate
2. Celsius
3. parasite
4. aquatic
5. bizarre
6. companion
7. biosphere
8. ecology
9. vulnerable
10. feat

Exercise 2
1. tolerance
2. repetitive
3. prominent
4. nucleus
5. coarse

Exercise 3
1. I
2. C
3. C
4. I
5. I
6. C
7. I
8. C
9. C
10. I
11. I
12. C
13. C
14. C
15. I
16. I
17. I
18. C
19. I
20. C

Reading Comprehension
Part A
1. F Protists have a high tolerance for **extreme** conditions.
2. T
3. F A protist splits its **own** nucleus in fission.
4. T
5. T

Part B
1. The protest could be comfortable in water that was 150 degrees Celsius.
2. Protists were the first life form on Earth.
3. A protists releases nitrogen gas.
4. It swims up to one and swallows it whole.
5. A protists undergoes the reproductive process of fission

Unit 8

Exercise 1
1. a
2. c
3. b
4. c
5. a

Exercise 2
1. hostile
2. dominate
3. misconception
4. culinary
5. medication
6. prescription
7. edible
8. peel
9. malnutrition
10. intake

Exercise 3
1. c
2. d
3. b
4. a
5. c

Exercise 4
1. I
2. C
3. C
4. C
5. I
6. C
7. C
8. I
9. I
10. I
11. C
12. I
13. I
14. C
15. C

Reading Comprehension
Part A
1. T
2. F The hostile **army** wanted to dominate and oppress the people.
3. T
4. F The doctor showed the woman a dense patch of **edible plants**.
5. F The woman gave the doctor a ceramic bowl to show **her thanks**.

Part B
1. He wanted to use a new medication to treat the sick people.
2. She thought bread and water would be enough for him.
3. He wanted her to increase her son's intake of vegetables.
4. He gave her a prescription for pain medicine.
5. He wanted her to help her son stay healthy.

Unit 9

Exercise 1
1. b
2. a
3. b
4. c
5. c

Exercise 2
1. c
2. a
3. d
4. c
5. b

Exercise 3
1. b
2. d
3. a
4. c
5. a

Exercise 4
1. C
2. I
3. C
4. I
5. C

Exercise 5
1. peninsula
2. diminish
3. dependence
4. drawbacks
5. proportion
6. components
7. impose
8. refuted
9. spectacular
10. benevolent

Reading Comprehension
Part A
1. F The mayor of Netherton **didn't want** Joseph to impose his radical fad on the town.
2. T
3. F The mayor of Wilton **couldn't refute** the fact that the machine had drawbacks.
4. T
5. T

Part B
1. A large proportion of the people worked in weaving.
2. Cloth made by hand will soon be obsolete.
3. If he bought the machine, the people would lose their jobs.
4. He realized the machine could bring money and prestige.
5. Nobody bought the poor cloth from Netherton anymore.

Unit 10

Exercise 1
1. b
2. a
3. c
4. a
5. a

Exercise 2
1. d
2. a
3. b
4. b
5. b
6. c
7. d
8. b
9. a
10. d

Exercise 3
1. C
2. C
3. I
4. I
5. C
6. I
7. C
8. C
9. I
10. I

Exercise 4
1. soy
2. precaution
3. Accountants
4. monetary
5. preliminary
6. saturated
7. financed
8. capitalist
9. indifferent
10. dedicate

Reading Comprehension

Part A
1. T
2. F   Bill was indifferent about the **company's** success.
3. F   Bill irrigated his crops as a precaution for the upcoming **dry** summer.
4. T
5. F   ...and **planted** soy and cabbage.

Part B
1. "You're crazy!"
2. Bill had contempt toward his job.
3. Bill was happy.
4. Buying land and tools
5. The simplicity of a life on a farm

Unit 11

Exercise 1
1. b
2. a
3. c
4. a
5. d

Exercise 2
1. biography
2. acute
3. aggression
4. virtue
5. narrated
6. partiality
7. outdated
8. legacy
9. notorious
10. compel

Exercise 3
1. I
2. C
3. I
4. C
5. C
6. I
7. C
8. I
9. C
10. I
11. I
12. C
13. I
14. C
15. I
16. C
17. C
18. I
19. C
20. C

Reading Comprehension
Part A
1. T
2. T
3. F It was inevitable that Beethoven would lose his **hearing** altogether.
4. T
5. F Beethoven's legacy lives on because great music **never becomes** outdated.

Part B
1. The young Beethoven developed a partiality for classical music.
2. He first learned to play the piano when he was five.
3. He began to cry.
4. His passion for music compelled him to keep performing.
5. It was one of the finest in history.

Unit 12

Exercise 1
1. c
2. a
3. b
4. c
5. a

Exercise 2
1. consecutive
2. masculine
3. compatible
4. muscular
5. undergraduate
6. tattoo
7. posture
8. symmetry
9. ignorance
10. crude

Exercise 3
1. C
2. C
3. I
4. C
5. C
6. C
7. I
8. C
9. I
10. C
11. I
12. I
13. C
14. C
15. C
16. I
17. C
18. I
19. I
20. C

Reading Comprehension
Part A
1. T
2. F John laughed at **Mark's** ignorance.
3. T
4. T
5. F John was an undergraduate who studied **history** and anthropology.

Part B
1. They were applauded for their hard work.
2. He thought he could build a good statue.
3. John told him what Tut looked like.
4. Mark conferred with John about every detail.
5. When we put our talents together, we are capable of greatness.

Unit 13

Exercise 1
1. a
2. b
3. a
4. a
5. b

Exercise 2
1. brook
2. consumption
3. pedestrians
4. escort
5. hound
6. faculty
7. spectators
8. facility
9. impersonal
10. considerate

Exercise 3
1. b
2. d
3. c
4. d
5. d

Exercise 4
1. hounds
2. crust
3. spectator
4. ornaments
5. criteria
6. sanctuary
7. faculty
8. heap
9. brook
10. entitle

Reading Comprehension
Part A
1. F Elvis possessed the criteria to be a **great racing dog**.
2. T
3. T
4. F In the interior the facility, there was a heap of **bones** and bread crusts for consumption.
5. T

Part B
1. His faculties were not as strong as they used to be.
2. Elvis was entitled to a better life.
3. He never lost a race in the northern hemisphere.
4. Elvis was escorted to a beautiful facility.
5. There was a sign on the external door that said, "Dogs Welcome!"

Unit 14

Exercise 1
1. c
2. a
3. c
4. b
5. a
6. b
7. a
8. d
9. b
10. a

Exercise 2
1. b
2. a
3. a
4. c
5. b

Exercise 3
1. I
2. I
3. C
4. C
5. C
6. C
7. I
8. I
9. C
10. C
11. C
12. I
13. I
14. C
15. C
16. C
17. C
18. I
19. C
20. C

Reading Comprehension
Part A
1. T
2. F At first, Sam is a **skeptic**. He thinks the assignment will be easy.
3. F When Sam goes into the kitchen, he can't read the newspaper.
4. T
5. F Without his sense of sight, Sam has worse **spatial** awareness and isn't able to **coordinate** his movements easily.

Part B
1. According to the teacher, the **premise** of the experiment is to help the students understand what it's like to be blind.
2. Sam realized how important hearing was for blind people.
3. Sam wasn't able to perform **simultaneous** activities because he had to make sure he was safe first.
4. Sam noticed that the bud seemed to be covered with **wax**.
5. It showed him sight was an asset that should be appreciated and taught him to revere the talents of blind people.

Unit 15

Exercise 1
1. c
2. b
3. c
4. d
5. a

Exercise 2
1. inferred
2. adequate
3. innate
4. facilitate
5. pouch
6. update
7. fleet
8. saturated
9. mast
10. inflated

Exercise 3
1. b
2. a
3. c
4. c
5. a
6. b
7. a
8. c
9. d
10. c

Exercise 4
1. I
2. I
3. I
4. C
5. C

Reading Comprehension
Part A
1. T
2. T
3. F When Ernest saw the man standing next to the mast, he decided to **help him out of his dilemma.**
4. T
5. F Ernest had the innate desire to **help others**.

Part B
1. There was an elaborate painting of a naval battle on the side of his boat.
2. Their clothes were saturated with seawater.
3. Ernest thought the boy was suffering from nausea.
4. There were several large fish in a pouch in the boat.
5. Ernest learned it better not to offer help unless it was asked for.

Unit 16

Exercise 1
1. d
2. c
3. a
4. b
5. b

Exercise 2
1. courtyard
2. chaotic
3. corresponded
4. cited
5. fraud

Exercise 4
1. C
2. I
3. C
4. I
5. C
6. C
7. I
8. C
9. C
10. I
11. C
12. I
13. I
14. C
15. I

Exercise 3
1. b
2. d
3. a
4. b
5. a

Reading Comprehension
Part A
1. F There is no archeological evidence that the Chinese actually made parachutes.
2. F A Da Vinci drawing of a parachute corresponds with modern parachute design.
3. T
4. F He used two umbrellas to restrict his speed as he traveled to the gound.
5. T

Part B
1. Sebastian used umbrellas because he had a small budget.
2. Sebastian thought that a parachute would restrict the jumper from gaining too much speed as they fell.
3. Sebastian jumped off a tall building on a French estate and landed safely in the courtyard.
4. Jean-Pierre was a proponent of using parachutes to jump out hot air balloons instead of using them to jump out of burning buildings.
5. Jean-Pierre first used the parachute when he had a chaotic experience and the balloon he was riding in burst.

Unit 17

Exercise 1
1. b
2. d
3. a
4. c
5. b

Exercise 2
1. a
2. c
3. b
4. b
5. b
6. a
7. c
8. c
9. a
10. b

Exercise 3
1. graduated
2. donor
3. tuition
4. stimulus
5. implicated
6. graffiti
7. chronic
8. discipline
9. gossip
10. terminate

Exercise 4
1. C
2. I
3. I
4. C
5. I
6. C
7. I
8. C
9. C
10. C
11. I
12. C
13. I
14. C
15. C

Reading Comprehension

Part A
1. F The principal hung the painting in front of the office as a stimulus for the students to play sports.
2. T
3. F Billy was implicated because a fellow student said she **saw him do it.**
4. T
5. F The principal threatened to terminate Billy's education if his parents didn't pay for the painting.

Part B
1. The principal said that Billy was a chronic liar.
2. His suspicion was that the tape from the security cameras would show who really did the crime.
3. The videotape showed another boy leaving graffiti on the painting, holding a knife by the shaft and stabbing it, then using the knife to sever the string that held it up.
4. The attorney suggested that the boy responsible needed discipline.
5. Billy said he wanted to major in law and became an attorney so he could be a guardian of justice like Mr. Meyers.

Unit 18

Exercise 1
1. d
2. a
3. c
4. a
5.c

Exercise 2
1. b
2. b
3. a
4. c
5. d
6. c
7. a
8. a
9. c
10. d

Exercise 3
1. b
2. b
3. d
4. b
5. a
6. d
7. c
8. a
9. a
10. c

Exercise 4
1. C
2. I
3. C
4. I
5. C

Reading Comprehension
Part A
1. T
2. F The prisoner was led from the **compound** to the **arena**.
3. F While he meditated, the soldier was **not** distracted by his opponent.
4. F The king gave the brave soldier amnesty.
5. T

Part B
1. The captive seemed like he was dumb because he was quiet.

2. Making captives fight one another was commonplace during the reign of the enemy king.
3. His opponent was skilled in the realm of sword fighting.
4. The soldier was nicked on the cheek.
5. The quiet soldier proved that peace can conquer violence.

Unit 19

Exercise 1
1. b
2. c
3. d
4. a
5. a

Exercise 2
1. secondhand
2. dock
3. distort
4. fore
5. accordingly
6. context
7. intricate
8. overlap
9. designate
10. grease

Exercise 3
1. C
2. C
3. I
4. I
5. C
6. I
7. I
8. C
9. I
10. I
11. C
12. C
13. C
14. I
15. C
16. C
17. I
18. C
19. I
20. C

Reading Comprehension

Part A
1. F Jane thought she would precipitate a disaster if she **made** her frequent mistakes.
2. T
3. F Jane put grease on the intricate **motor's gears**.
4. T
5. T

Part B
1. She had to steer the boat back to the dock to find help.
2. She pulled up the anchor with all of her might.
3. They painted the name on the fore of the ship
4. She was trying to offset the wind.
5. It was to prove to her that she was capable and important.

Unit 20

Exercise 1
1. b
2. b
3. a
4. c
5. a

Exercise 2
1. viral
2. antibiotic
3. database
4. ratio
5. phase
6. spiral
7. magnet
8. input
9. prevalent
10. immune

Exercise 3
1. prevalent
2. phase
3. viral
4. antibiotics
5. complement
6. input
7. database
8. pinch
9. metabolism
10. spiral

Exercise 4
1. C
2. I
3. C
4. C
5. I
6. C
7. I
8. C
9. C
10. I

Reading Comprehension
Part A
1. T
2. F Chips express the aggregate number of immune and **infected** cells in a ratio.
3. T
4. T
5. F Putting **microchips** in humans is becoming more prevalent.

Part B
1. The special magnet copies the chip's data.
2. Microchips hold about the same amount of data as most computers.
3. The next phase of the process involves putting it underneath the person's skin.
4. Microchips scan the patient's body.
5. Medicine and computer technology complement each other.

Unit 21

Exercise 1
1. a
2. a
3. a
4. c
5. b

Exercise 2
1. b
2. d
3. b
4. c
5. c
6.d
7.d
8.c
9.b
10.a

Exercise 3
1. I
2. I
3. I
4. I
5. C
6. C
7. I
8. I
9. C
10. I
11. C
12. C
13. C
14. I
15. I
16. C
17. I
18. I
19. C
20. C

Reading Comprehension.

Part A
1. F The girls looked like clones, **and** they used **the same** colloquial language.
2. F ... Katie was **a linguist** and Alice ...
3. T
4. F Alice was astounded when she saw Katie wearing **nice clothes**.
5. T

Part B
1. Alice wasn't interested in French.
2. Alice felt very messy next to her.
3. In the past they'd always told each other everything in detail.
4. Before their birthday, they'd talk all night long.
5. It's totally plausible for twins to have different interests.

Unit 22

Exercise 1
1. a
2. b
3. b
4. c
5. a

Exercise 2
1. manufactures
2. mechanisms
3. administration
4. cholesterol
5. deceptive
6. explicit
7. coalition
8. prone
9. framework
10. straightforward

Exercise 3
1. C
2. C
3. I
4. C
5. I
6. C
7. I
8. C
9. C
10. C
11. I
12. C
13. C
14. I
15. C
16. I
17. C
18. I
19. C
20. I

Reading Comprehension
Part A
1. F ... **manufactured drugs to treat** diabetes and high cholesterol.
2. T
3. T
4. T
5. F After the company minimized **air pollution**, the motto became apt.

Part B
1. "Make the Earth a better place."
2. Jack stood up to give a speech.
3. We can fix things if we all work together.
4. The workers threatened to quit.
5. Since I can't afford to lose all my workers, I guess we'll just have to fix things.

Unit 23

Exercise 1
1. b
2. d
3. a
4. b
5. a
6. c
7. d
8. c
9. d
10. a

Exercise 2
1. d
2. c
3. b
4. b
5. d
6. a
7. b
8. c
9. a
10. c

Exercise 3
1. a
2. c
3. c
4. a
5. b

Exercise 4
1. crescent
2. roamed
3. craters
4. breadth
5. fragment
6. atom
7. embedded
8. solitary
9. radiates
10. status

Reading Comprehension
Part A
1. F ...through the debris of broken **asteroids**.
2. T
3. F The **tail** shined with...
4. T
5. T

Part B
1. While roaming through the gloom of the galaxy, the little rock felt sad.
2. The moons had craters and shiny crescents.
3. The circumference of the planet was hundreds of times larger than the breadth of the small rock.
4. The little fragment of rock was filled with despair because he was surrounded by beauty and greatness, yet he was just a small and ugly rock.
5. The tail looked like a galactic cape.

Unit 24

Exercise 1

1. a
2. d
3. c
4. b
5. a

Exercise 2

1. employs
2. expelled
3. furnished
4. hygiene
5. lease
6. mend
7. personnel
8. plumbing
9. trendy
10. utility

Exercise 3

1. I
2. C
3. C
4. I
5. C
6. I
7. I
8. I
9. C
10. C
11. I
12. C
13. I
14. C
15. C
16. I
17. I
18. C
19. C
20. C

Reading Comprehension

Part A

1 F If the tenants didn't pay the **lease**, the landlord could not pay his **mortgage** and…
2. T
3. T
4. F The **carpenter** mended…
5. T

Part B

1. In addition to dressers, the tenants furnished some of the apartments with new beds and chairs.
2. If the landlord did not conform to the city's mandatory hygienic standards, his tenants would have to leave by the end of the month.
3. He had requested an extension, but the city denied it.
4. The tenant who had worked for the city's utilities repaired the building's plumbing.
5. When they were done, all of the people dispersed, and the landlord went home to rest.

Unit 25

Exercise 1
1. a
2. b
3. b
4. c
5. a

Exercise 2
1. canyon
2. fatigue
3. stereotype
4. primitive
5. trail
6. aesthetic
7. termites
8. twig
9. creek
10. welfare

Exercise 3
1. a
2. c
3. d
4. a
5. c
6. d
7. b
8. a
9. a
10. d

Exercise 4
1. twigs
2. sticky
3. primitive
4. primates
5. fatigue

Reading Comprehension
Part A
1. F The executive **did not care** about…
2. T
3. T
4. F The executive walked up the **steep** incline of the jungle's hills.
5. F The executive's stereotype of the primate was **wrong**.

Part B
1. The honey on the twig that made it sticky enough to capture termites.

2. Fatigue and hunger weakened him.
3. Because he had a bias against the primitive ways of the monkey, he had gone hungry.
4. He used the twig like it was a drill.
5. He never perceived that his arrogant attitude was the cause of all his problems.

Unit 26

Exercise 1
1. b
2. a
3. b
4. c
5. a

Exercise 2
1. globe
2. behalf
3. rite
4. overview
5. provided
6. loaf
7. inward
8. relevant
9. oracles
10. orbit

Exercise 3
1. a
2. b
3. d
4. a
5. c

Exercise 4
1. previous
2. oracle
3. horizontal
4. preview
5. loaf
6. inward
7. hum
8. provide
9. stall
10. glacier

Reading Comprehension
Part A
1. T
2. T
3. F In Dano's summary, he told Cosmo to keep his body horizontal against the winds of the Pacific Ocean.
4. F **Cosmo** flapped his wings and orbited the globe.
5. F Cosmo hummed a tune while he flew and enjoyed the view.

Part B
1. Cosmo's inward thoughts about falling were no longer relevant.
2. Dano told Cosmo that the mountain tops will look like loaves of bread.
3. "I'll do my best."
4. The rivers of the world would look like pieces of blue string.
5. He declared Cosmo a man.

Unit 27

Exercise 1
1. a
2. c
3. c
4. b
5. a

Exercise 2
1. therapy
2. biological
3. fantasy
4. adapt
5. cellular
6. rigid
7. dynamic
8. pioneer
9. sequence
10. revived

Exercise 3
1. C
2. C
3. I
4. I
5. C
6. C
7. I
8. C
9. I
10. C
11. C
12. I
13. I
14. I
15. C
16. I
17. C
18. I
19. I
20. C

Reading Comprehension
Part A
1. F Internal organ transplants were a fantasy **before** 1954.
2. F **Dr. Murray** was a pioneer of new surgical procedures.
3. T
4. T
5. T

Part B
1. Robert's working kidney was substituted for Richard's bad one.
2. They had the exact same biological traits and cellular features.
3. Doctors prescribed physical therapy to revive Richard's strength.
4. The surgeons made minimal cuts in the twins' sides.
5. Richard was a healthy, happy person.

Unit 28

Exercise 1
1. b
2. b
3. c
4. a
5. a

Exercise 2
1. b
2. c
3. d
4. a
5. b
6. a
7. a
8. b
9. d
10. c

Exercise 3
1. I
2. C
3. I
4. I
5. C
6. C
7. I
8. I
9. I
10. C
11. C
12. C
13. I
14. C
15. I
16. C
17. C
18. I
19. C
20. C

Reading Comprehension

Part A
1. T
2. T
3. F If Joe wrote an autobiography, he would write **that this was the happiest day of his life.**
4. T
5. F When he opened the door, he saw a beautiful woman.

Part B
1. Joe thought the naughty neighborhood children were playing a trick on him.
2. He took out some stationery to write a letter to the zoo.
3. He bought healthy food for them.
4. He probed Joe to learn why he spent his money on the zoo instead of on himself.
5. He would describe this day as the happiest day of his life.

Unit 29

Exercise 1
1. a
2. b
3. a
4. b
5. a

Exercise 2
1. tusks
2. antique
3. monarch
4. Majesty
5. applicants
6. register
7. authentic
8. refund
9. fossil
10. artifact

Exercise 3
1. d
2. a
3. b
4. d
5. b

Exercise 4
1. tusk
2. authentic
3. recruit
4. punctual
5. chronology
6. fossil
7. excerpt
8. lyric
9. epic
10. renown

Reading Comprehension
Part A
1. T
2. T
3. F **Jen** bumped into the fossil of an authentic elephant tusk.
4. F Jen was chosen because she was friendly, punctual, and had **a great attitude**.
5. T

Part B
1. Jen hoped that the rest of the tour would go better.
2. Jen wanted to talk about the chronology of Ancient Egypt.
3. She sneezed and tore a page of the epic.
4. Jen thought she was a horrible tour guide.
5. Hard work

Unit 30

Exercise 1
1. b
2. b
3. b
4. a
5. c
6. a
7. b
8. a
9. b
10. b

Exercise 2
1. sociable
2. tramped
3. crafted
4. rigged
5. merged

Exercise 3
1. d
2. c
3. a
4. a
5. b
6. b
7. c
8. a
9. d
10. d

Exercise 4
1. I
2. C
3. I
4. I
5. C
6. C
7. I
8. C
9. C
10. I

Reading Comprehension
Part A
1. T
2. F ... by how **high the water had risen.**
3. T
4. T
5. F ... reunion with **her dog and cow.**

Part B
1. The man turned into a hybrid of a human and a fish.
2. She was overwhelmed by how high the water had risen.
3. He asked for the first living thing that crosses the bridge.
4. She shivered because she realized that he had taken advantage of her innocence and rigged a trap for her.
5. He called her a "crook."